T0132687

Leadership in the Life Sciences

The healthcare professionals who save and extend our lives are helpless without the medicines and technologies that have revolutionised medical care. But the industry that invents, makes and provides these indispensable tools is transforming under the pressure of ageing populations, globalisation and revolutions in biological and information technology. How this industry adapts and evolves is vitally important to every one of us.

This book looks inside the heads and hearts of the people who lead the global pharmaceutical and medical technology industry. It describes how they make sense of their markets and the wider life sciences economy. It reveals what they have learned about how to lead large, complex organisations to compete in dynamic, global markets.

Leadership in the Life Sciences is essential reading for anyone working in or with the pharmaceutical and medical technology industry and its halo of supporting companies. Written as ten succinct lessons, it gives the reader unique insight into what the industry's leaders are thinking. Covering topics from leadership to organisational culture, from change management to digital disruption and from competitive strategy to value-creation, each chapter distils the accumulated wisdom of those who lead the complex and turbulent life sciences industry.

Brian D. Smith is an academic, author and advisor in the area of competitive strategy and has been described as the world's leading authority on the evolution of the life sciences sector. He has 20 years of research experience at Europe's leading business schools, has published over 300 books, papers and articles and provides strategy advice to many global companies in the pharmaceutical and medical technology sectors. He is an adjunct professor at SDA Bocconi, Milan and a visiting professor at the University of Hertfordshire, UK. This follows on from 20 years' experience in the pharma and medical device industry, first as a research chemist and then in an ascending series of marketing roles.

Leadership in the Life Sciences

Ten Lessons from the C-Suite of Pharmaceutical and Medical Technology Companies

Brian D. Smith

Routledge
Taylor & Francis Group
LONDON AND NEW YORK

First published 2020
by Routledge
2 Park Square, Milton Park, Abingdon, Oxon OX14 4RN

and by Routledge
52 Vanderbilt Avenue, New York, NY 10017

Routledge is an imprint of the Taylor & Francis Group, an informa
business

British Library Cataloguing-in-Publication Data
A catalogue record for this book is available from the British
Library

Library of Congress Cataloging-in-Publication Data
Names: Smith, Brian D. (Brian David), 1961– author.
Title: Leadership in the life sciences : ten lessons from the
C-suite of pharmaceutical and medical technology companies /
Brian D. Smith.
Description: Abingdon, Oxon ; New York, NY :
Routledge, 2020. | Includes index.
Identifiers: LCCN 2019016477 (print) | LCCN 2019019531
(ebook) | ISBN 9780429022319 (eBook) | ISBN 9780367077181
(hardback : alk. paper)
Subjects: LCSH: Pharmaceutical industry—Management. |
Medical care. | Medical technology. | Leadership.
Classification: LCC HD9665.5 (ebook) | LCC HD9665.5 .S589
2020 (print) | DDC 615.1068/4—dc23
LC record available at https://lccn.loc.gov/2019016477

ISBN: 978-0-367-07718-1 (hbk)
ISBN: 978-0-429-02231-9 (ebk)

Typeset in Gill Sans
by codeMantra

For Lindsay, Eleanor, Catherine and Rosalind

Contents

Acknowledgements

I would like to thank all of those who supported me in writing this book. In particular, I'd like to thank the CEOs and others who made time to answer my questions:

Gabriel Baertschi, Chairman of the Corporate Executive Board and Chief Executive Officer, Grünenthal GmbH

Patrice Baudry, Executive Vice President, LEO Pharma

Roland Diggelmann, former Chief Executive Officer, Roche Diagnostics

Deborah Dunsire, Chief Executive Officer, Lundbeck

Jane Griffiths, Global Head, Actelion

Allan Hillgrove, Member of the Board of Managing Directors, Boehringer Ingelheim

Lars Fruergaard Jørgensen, President and Chief Executive Officer at Novo Nordisk

Jeremy M. Levin, Chairman and Chief Executive Officer, Ovid Therapeutics

Meinrad Lugan, Member of the Board at B. Braun Melsungen AG

Russell Mably, Chief Commercial Officer, Corin

Louise Makin, Chief Executive Officer, BTG plc

Peter Martin, Chief Operating Officer, Norgine

Yukio Matsui, Chief Commercial Officer, Astellas Pharma

Will McGuire, President and Chief Executive Officer at Second Sight Medical Products

Stephen Moran, Global Head of Strategy, Novartis

Kieran Murphy, President and Chief Executive Officer, GE Healthcare

Namal Nawana, Chief Executive Officer, Smith & Nephew

Michel Pettigrew, former President and Chief Operating Officer, Ferring

Peter Stein, Chief Executive Officer, Norgine

Jeroen Tas, Chief Innovation and Strategy Officer and Member of the
    Executive Committee at Royal Philips
Jean-Christophe Tellier, Chief Executive Officer, UCB
Andrew Thompson, Chief Executive Officer at Proteus Health
Maurits Wolleswinkel, Head of Portfolio and Chief Strategy Officer,
    Elekta

I also thank the large number of people who made these interviews
possible. From senior executives who effected introductions, to media relations people who coordinated the interviews, to personal
assistants who arranged the meetings, this book was made possible
by these very busy people giving up their time to help me. My thanks
extend also to the many who tried to set up interviews for me but
who, for various reasons, were unable to. I am immensely grateful
to you all.

Preface

This book is written for those who share my fascination for and love of the industry that makes medicines, medical devices, diagnostics and other medical technology. From my first job as a research technician synthesising medicines, to my current one as a research professor analysing business models, I've been enthralled by how this industry harnesses science to save, improve and extend lives. If you feel the same, then this book is meant for you.

Although I am the writer of this book, there is a sense in which I am not its only author. The book is a construction of many layers. Its foundations are my more than 20 years of academic research and curiosity to understand the industry. Its structural frame is the many interviews, articles and presentations by CEOs and C-level leaders in the industry that I was able to read and watch as I tried to make sense of our industry's complex nature. Its architecture is a product of how I convey that complexity as a meaningful vision. But its aesthetic design comes very much from interviews with the 22 Life Science Leaders who were kind enough to talk to me as part of my research.

This book includes many references to what my interviewees said. I have tried very hard to fairly represent the content and context of their words, but I have not quoted them directly. Our conversations were wide ranging, informal and often unstructured. Quoting verbatim but incompletely would have risked compromising their meaning, as well as making the book much longer and harder to read. I believe I've communicated their meaning accurately, but I have edited and sometimes paraphrased their words for clarity. Readers should not take what I've written as direct quotations from my interviews. And, of course, the opinions expressed in the book are mine alone.

I have written this book for a time-poor audience that might read it whilst travelling or facing other distractions. Each chapter is relatively short, about the length of a magazine article and, unlike most of my other published work, I've chosen not to support my points with citations and references. If any readers would like to follow up on what I've written, I invite them to contact me directly and I'll point them towards further reading. I've also tried to write the chapters as self-contained units, so that readers can read them in any order that interests them. The exception to this is Lesson 1, which contains ideas that I return to throughout the book.

However you choose to read *Leadership in the Life Sciences*, I would ask you to bear in mind the gap it tries to fill. There are many books about leadership but, despite their various approaches, they mostly share two assumptions. Firstly, since they are written to apply to leadership in any industry, they assume that leadership doesn't vary with industry context. Secondly, since they are generally prescriptive, they mostly assume that there is a best way to lead. Neither assumption fits with my experience, so I have tried to write a book that is different in two ways. First of all, it is industry specific. It makes no claims to validity outside of the life sciences industry but it is, I hope, an accurate description of leadership in pharma, medtech and related sectors. Secondly, it is descriptive rather than prescriptive. It describes what I think my industry leaders have learned, but it leaves it up to readers if they wish to accept or ignore these lessons. By writing a descriptive book specific to this fascinating industry, I hope it will be valuable to those who have an interest in, and perhaps aspire to, leadership in the life sciences.

Thank you in anticipation for giving your time to this book. I am always delighted to receive praise, criticisms or questions from my readers.

Professor Brian D. Smith
brian.smith@pragmedic.com
April 2019

1 The life sciences industry really is exceptional

Is the life sciences industry really different from any other? The question is important because, if it is exceptional, then we might expect leadership in pharmaceutical, medical technology and related companies to be different from that in other businesses. Conversely, if the reverse is true and the life sciences industry is really no different from others, or if it differs only in minor details, then the plethora of theories, books and articles about leadership will apply as well to this sector as they do to any other. So, the question has important, practical implications and it was the first one I asked when I sat down with my interviewees.

My question, and the supplementary questions that followed it, were designed to cut through the bias towards exceptionalism that one sees commonly amongst business people. Management researchers are familiar with and sometimes weary of executives who begin their answers with some version of the phrase, "You see, our industry is unique and not like any other". Typically, they then go on to describe a company that faces very similar challenges and arrives at very similar solutions to most other companies. Such genuine differences as they do describe are often no more than variations on a theme, such as exactly where low-cost competition comes from or the causes and consequences of rapid technological and social change. Like any other researcher, I had expected my interviewees to start from this position of exceptionalism.

It was refreshing and pleasantly surprising that the leaders of life science companies I interviewed almost always began with an opposite, unexceptional approach. At a fundamental level, they told me, they face the same challenges of understanding and addressing customer needs as their colleagues operating in other markets. Equally, their solutions could be resolved down to choices about how to focus scarce resources to optimise risk-adjusted return on investment. From that very high-level perspective, their job was not different from that of any other CEO.

However, once past these elementary parallels, they began to describe ways in which their situation and strategies were noticeably and importantly different from companies not operating in the life sciences market. The interviewees were often well placed to see these differences: some had worked in a variety of other sectors; some currently held board positions outside the life sciences industry; and all of them showed the breadth and depth of general business knowledge that you might expect to find in the C-suite. They had all considered this question before and were able to give thoughtful, substantive answers.

As is usually the case in qualitative research interviews, the answers appeared at first to be a flood of personal, individual observations, each couched in the interviewee's own vocabulary and illustrated with case-specific examples. To use an information technology metaphor, their answers were "noisy" and the "signals" were weak. During analysis, however, this amorphous mass of data crystallised into four distinct but related factors, four ways in which the life sciences industry can be said to differ significantly from other industries. As I will describe, these four differences – peculiarities or idiosyncrasies of the industry might be better descriptions – each has its origins in the specific social and technological context of the life sciences industry and important implications for how its leaders lead. They are, in the jargon of my academic speciality, selection pressures faced by leaders in this industry. That is, leadership traits in the sector are the result of adaptation to these four factors, which cumulatively favour some leadership behaviours and discriminate against others.

Difference 1: The social contract between the life sciences industry and society

As Lars Fruergaard Jørgensen eloquently put it, at the overlap of health, science and business, there is bound to be emotion. In the words of Namal Nawana, medical technology touches people's lives when they are at their most vulnerable. The products and services provided by the life sciences industry often are a matter of life and death. Even when they are not concerned with life threatening conditions, they have a very direct, viscerally-felt influence on the lives of patients and their families. And the group "patients and families" includes almost all of us. As Jane Griffiths put it, every one of our lives, or that of someone we love, has been or will be affected by this industry. Not all industries can make that claim and even those that can, such as utility companies, are not as emotionally salient as the life sciences industry.

This pervasive and prominent role that the life sciences industry plays in society, especially but not only in developed economies, has led to a special kind of relationship between the industry and society in general, one that is often described as a social contract. The industry's side of this agreement is that it will provide innovative technologies to save, prolong and improve lives. From vaccines to heart valves, the industry fulfils this side of the social contract in spades. When we are healthy, we tend to take this for granted but it only takes a bout of illness, an accident or a life event such as pregnancy for the industry's contribution to society to fall into sharp focus in the foreground of our lives. Of course, many would hope for more from this social contract; access to innovative medicines and technology is still a long way from universal and many medical needs remain unmet. But one only needs to compare our lives with those of our grandparents to appreciate what the life sciences industry has, in fact, contributed to our lives and to society in general.

In return for these evident benefits, society grants special privileges to the life sciences industry. Much of the basic science on which the industry is built comes not from its own discoveries but from publicly funded academic research. In most advanced economies, the large majority of the industry's revenue stream comes from publicly funded or supported healthcare systems. Many societies have pricing schemes, formal and otherwise, that recognise that medical innovation is sustainable only if the financial returns are adequate. Intellectual property rules for the industry, especially in pharmaceuticals, are made to safeguard these returns. Regulation, although aimed primarily at safety, is co-created between the industry and governments with the effect of protecting the former from low-quality competitors. And, when governments devise industrial strategies to support particular sectors, the life sciences industry is always one of those favoured. There are many ways in which the life sciences market is not a free market or "perfect" in an economist's sense of the term. In effect, society has agreed to help life science companies make money out of illness and distress because we want the benefits that flow from that arrangement.

The life sciences industry is not the only one to operate in an imperfect market with a special relationship to society. The defence sector, for example, is similarly distorted and for analogous reasons. The business of food and agriculture is notoriously politicised, regulated and managed to maintain supply and "food security". The education sector is, to a large degree, dominated by the government customers who set its direction. But none can be said to have the same pervasive and prominent emotional connection with society that the life sciences industry has created. In a real way, the industry can be seen as much as a social mission as an economic enterprise. This social contract between the industry and society means that expectations of it are higher than for others and have a strong moral component. It also means that the people who choose to work in the industry are often driven by higher motives as well as financial rewards. As we will see in later chapters, this influences the way its leaders must and do lead.

Difference 2: The complexity of value creation and value definition

Every market has a demand side, the customers whose needs define what is and is not valuable, and a supply side, the companies who find and deliver ways of meeting those needs and so create value in the eyes of the customer. When we discuss the relative complexity of a market, we are talking of the aggregate complexity of both demand and supply. Almost all advanced industries can claim to be complex in an absolute sense. But, relative to other industries and their markets, the life sciences can reasonably claim to be exceptionally complex in both demand and supply and, without doubt, it is exceptionally complex overall.

The demand side complexity of the life sciences industry is the result of human health being intricate, our approaches to managing health being convoluted and our political systems being Byzantine, in both senses of that term. There are more than 100,000 known diseases, divided into four main classes (infectious, hereditary, deficiency and physiological) that are spread across many distinct therapy areas which correspond, very roughly, to our biological systems such as cardiovascular and central nervous systems. Add to this all the possible injuries and conditions that, strictly speaking, are not illnesses, and the market for pharmaceutical and medical technology products is revealed as not a single, homogenous market but an enormous, interconnected hive of markets.

In addition to this medical complexity, the healthcare systems through which the industry reaches its customers are enormously varied in what they treat, how they treat and how they are funded.

As a global industry, the life sciences industry has to address every kind of healthcare system from the United States' insurance-based, payment-for-service model that offers the most advanced treatments to those who can afford it, to the socialised, universal care systems of Europe, to the out-of-pocket, bare-bones provision in some emerging markets. Added to this is the third dimension of politics, which shapes how countries interpret the social contract with the industry and how they choose to regulate it. In every country in the world, health-care is a politicised issue, which leads to variation between and often within countries. Even for firms that choose to narrow their disease and geographical focus, the market is a horribly fragmented three-dimensional matrix of clinical, economic and political issues. The truly global companies have to engage with the full scope of this complexity. Will McGuire neatly summed it up saying that, in this market, it is not as simple as inventing a great product that sells; reimbursement and health economic issues, which are based in political choices, are now as important as technological and clinical ones.

The supply side complexity of the industry is the result of the breadth and depth of both its physical and social technologies and the complex networks of organisations that are needed to create and deliver value. In innovative life science companies, the physical technology involved – the pharmacology, engineering and other applications of physical sciences – is often at the very edge of our knowledge. In pharmaceu-ticals, advanced therapies are now rarely simple, small molecules and are more often massive protein molecules or cell and gene therapies. In medical devices, traditional materials are being displaced by advanced polymers and composites, whilst in medical technologies connection to the "internet of things" is rapidly becoming the default option.

At the same time, traditional pharma/medtech divisions are eroding as value is created by the aggregation of several technologies. As Yukio Matsui points out, the technology involved in meeting clinical needs is now often a combination of complementary services, devices and medicines. Alongside these advances in physical technology are par-allel advances social technology. That is, in the applications of social sciences such as economics and sociology. The most prominent of these is the development of health economics to understand the value of treatments, but firms also employ ethnographers, sociologists and data scientists to create and deliver value.

The corollary of this increasing depth and breadth of both physical and social technology is that it is now relatively rare for healthcare value to be delivered by a single, vertically integrated firm. More often, value is now created by a so-called "holobiont", a network of organisations, from universities to contract manufacturers to the traditional life science company, with different but complementary assets and capabilities. As Jean-Christophe Tellier puts it, the complexity of the life sciences value chain, from basic science and discovery to marketing and support of patients and professionals, is a defining characteristic of the industry. His choice of the word "complex" is important, because the industry is not complicated like an airliner, it is complex like a rain forest. In complicated systems, the many different components remain the same, always behave the same way and the outcome of any action is predictable. In complex systems, the many different components change constantly as they adapt to each other and outcomes cannot be predicted. The life sciences industry is complex, like a rain forest, not complicated, like an airliner.

Other industries are complex, of course. The software industry has many different applications. The entertainment industry is characterised by holobionts, as you can observe when you watch the first few minutes of any movie. The social media industry combines social and physical technologies. In quantum computing, the hardware industry is operating at the limits of our knowledge. But no other industry deals with anything as intricate as human health. Other industries have convoluted supply chains but few have the symbiosis that exists between, for example, academic medical research and the life sciences industry. Many industries supplement their core technological expertise with, for instance, economic modelling, but it is hard to find any that need to demonstrate the value created across the customer's lifetime.

Taken as a whole, the combined complexity of the demand and supply sides of the life sciences industry is exceptional. This means that the twin challenges of any business – understanding how the customers define value and coordinating activity to create and deliver that value – are exceptionally difficult. This aggregate complexity makes it harder to be successful and easier to make catastrophic errors. As with the social contract, this complexity must and does influence how leaders in the life sciences industry do their job.

Difference 3: The magnitude and longevity of risk

All businesses are risk-management businesses. The differences between them are the size of the assets at risk, the level of risk and the period over which that risk must be borne. It would be simplistic to compare the life sciences industry with businesses that involve small investments and bear low risk for short periods such as, say, the restaurant business. However, even if we compare the life sciences industry with other capital intensive, long-term industries, such as automobiles or civil engineering, the risk associated with developing an innovative medical treatment is exceptional. Allan Hillgrove drew out the implications of this very well when he said the combination of size of investment, timescale and level of risk mean that leaders in this industry need to take a much longer perspective on planning.

The cost of bringing a new medicine or medical technology to market is very large, but even this does not tell the full story of what is at risk. The figure often cited for a new drug's development cost is $2.7 billion, a broad, averaged estimate from the Tufts Centre. The equivalent figure for a new medical device or technology is impossible to define, since the category is so much wider and innovation tends to be more incremental, but it is certainly in the range from tens to hundreds of millions. However, even these large figures are too small to realistically describe the magnitude of the industry's risk. When calculating a return on investment, it is necessary to consider all of the assets at risk. These go far beyond development cost and must include intangible assets, such as the firm's reputation with customers, investors and partners. If a drug or device fails in development or at launch, it erodes the asset of trust in the firm's capabilities. As Patrice Baudry pointed out, in this industry it is particularly important to be seen as a reliable, competent partner. In the case of a drug or device failing after launch, the financial and reputational liability can run into billions. For example, Merck payed around $5 billion to settle its Vioxx liabilities and, at the time of writing, Johnson & Johnson's Ethicon is embroiled in liability cases concerning the hundreds of thousands of women who received its vaginal mesh. When all tangible and intangible assets at risk are considered, the magnitude of risk in the life sciences industry does appear to be amongst the largest of any industry. As Louise Makin made clear, to work in this business you need to have an appetite for risk.

The second factor making the risk profile of the life sciences industry exceptional is the level of risk and uncertainty, the former being predictable and manageable, the latter being neither of those. In any business, the ultimate source of risk and uncertainty is imperfect knowledge and so it is closely correlated to the complexity of the industry and its social and technological environment. In the life sciences industry, the most prominent and visible artefacts of risk and uncertainty are product failures, the ultimate cause of which is imperfect knowledge of the technological environment.

In simple terms, the vast amount we don't know about how the human body works can hide innumerable risks and uncertainties. In pharmaceuticals, various estimates suggest that each launched drug is the sole survivor of many thousands of initial candidates. In the more incremental development process of medical devices and technology, it is less common for products to fail and more common that many smaller but costly technical experiments must be tried before an effective, incremental advance is made. And, as the Vioxx and vaginal mesh examples demonstrate, even a successful launch cannot be considered the end of this technical, scientific risk. Real world, post-launch data can reveal failures that were invisible in development.

Traditionally less prominent than these technical risks, but becoming more salient, are risks and uncertainties associated with the social environment, including regulatory and commercial risk. The former, that the product will not gain and retain regulatory approval, is the result of increasingly complex and demanding regulatory requirements. The naïve observer might assume that, since these regulations are published, they are known and create little risk. But regulatory professionals recognise that the complexity of regulation has led to ambiguity, and therefore risk. Like technical risk, regulatory risk does not end at launch, as firms who have lost regulatory approval for manufacturing systems can attest. Commercial risk, that the product may not achieve its intended returns, has traditionally included risks around indeterminate market size, competitive intensity and operating costs. These risks remain but, increasingly, commercial risk now also includes access risk – that the product may not be considered good value by payers, and so not be paid for by state or private insurance systems. When technical risks (that the product may not work or be considered safe and effective) are combined with commercial risks (that the product may not make a worthwhile return), the high level of risk inherent in the life sciences industry becomes starkly apparent.

As if very large assets bearing high levels of risk and uncertainty were not sufficient to justify the industry's claim to exceptionalism, these factors are also magnified by timescale. Since risk and uncertainty are the result of imperfect knowledge, and since the further we look into the future the more imperfect our knowledge becomes, risk and uncertainty are amplified as life science companies plan ahead. Meinrad

Lugan made clear the necessity to think of product life cycles lasting decades not years, because of the time it takes to develop a medical technology, for it to become adopted into practice and for it to be superseded by other technologies. Similarly, Allan Hillgrove described the pharmaceutical industry as a 40-year cycle in which today's profits, which are the result of investments 20 years ago, are being invested to generate returns 20 years from now. These decades-long planning cycles amplify all of the risk categories discussed above. Looking that far into the future, our knowledge of what the technological and social environments will become grows inevitably less certain. As a result, the risk that our products may not be successful, either technically or economically, increases.

The life sciences industry is not the only one to place big bets, to have high levels of risk or to work in long cycles. The automobile industry measures development costs in billions and risks similar reputational assets. Capital projects, such as power stations, have long lifetimes, although these are often underwritten by governments. Any new venture, especially using advanced technology, has high levels of risk. But it is hard to think of any industry other than the life sciences that combines such large assets at risk over such extended timescales whilst operating in technological and social environments that are so inherently risky. As with the social contract and complexity, I mentioned earlier, the life sciences industry can reasonably claim to be unusual to the point of exceptionality in this respect. And, once again, the industry's magnitude and longevity of risk acts as a selection pressure, shaping the behaviours of its leaders. A Life Science Leader who did not understand and manage risk would become extinct very quickly.

Difference 4: The composition of the workforce

There are no businesses that do not depend on the knowledge, skills and attributes of their employees. But not all industries have the same kind of workforce. It would be naïve to equate, for example, the workforce of a packing warehouse, such as Amazon, with that of a law firm. The composition of the workforce of any industry is characterised by three dimensions: the level of expertise demanded of its most qualified people, the range of different expertise it requires to compete, and the proportion of its workforce who are highly educated and skilled. The life sciences industry lies towards the higher extreme on all three of these dimensions and so can reasonably claim to be exceptional in the composition of its workforce. Or, to use the crisper, to-the-point description given by Deborah Dunsire, to be a world class life science company requires a very high concentration of intellectual capital across a remarkably large range of disciplines.

The expertise level of the life sciences industry, measured in the qualifications and experience of its most expert people, is one of its most obvious characteristics. There are few industries in which the most specialised employees are comparable, in experience and reputation, with the leading academic authorities in the field, yet this is commonplace amongst the disease area specialists in the pharmaceutical industry and among material scientists and design engineers in medical devices. Nor is this expertise restricted to only a small number of scientific specialists within the company. As Maurits Wolleswinkel stridently pointed out, what makes his business special is that it requires a high degree of knowledge intensity across not only technical functions but also across other areas, such as medical affairs, manufacturing and marketing. Kieran Murphy also illustrated this, pointing out that the provision of integrated solutions, rather than discrete products, to a hospital required not only product expertise but an expertise in hospital workflow and design that was superior to that found in most hospitals. This breadth of expertise is also, in part, a function of the industry's regulatory environment, which demands and inspects for compliance to high standards across the entire value chain, from development to marketing and post-marketing.

In addition to the high level of expertise of its most qualified people and the range of different expertise required by the industry, a third defining characteristic of the life sciences industry is the proportion of its workforce that is highly educated and skilled. This is perhaps most evident in functional areas in which, in other industries, lower levels of skills and formal qualification are common. In sales and marketing in life science companies, for instance, it is routine for sales staff to be science graduates and it is not uncommon to find PhDs. Even relatively junior roles in manufacturing, clinical development and administration are typically required to maintain professional qualifications to meet compliance demands. Overall, the proportion of those working in the life sciences industry without higher level qualifications is low compared to most other industries. Even this assessment understates the case because of the extensive practice of outsourcing and collaboration in the industry. If collaborations with universities and hospitals and outsourcing to specialist sub-contractors were included, the composition of the industry's workforce is even more strongly skewed towards highly qualified and trained experts.

None of this is to say that other industries employ only a few bright people alongside a majority of unqualified, unskilled labour. Most high added-value industries, from jet-engine manufacture to fashion, rely on very skilled workforces. But, even using a fair comparison with other knowledge-intensive industries, the life sciences industry's combination of a great proportion of highly expert workers across the width of its value chain supports the case that it is exceptional.

Just as with the social contract, complexity and risk, this workforce composition has meaningful implications for its leadership. Leaders who behave in a manner better suited to a less-expert workforce would quickly fail and be replaced by those whose habits enable a workforce of experts. In this way, the life science's workforce shapes its leaders at least as much as the other way around.

A confluence of exceptional factors

I began this chapter questioning the exceptionalness of the life sciences industry. In the research for this book, I asked the question very directly of my interviewees, who were well qualified to answer. Attempting to give balanced, objective assessments, they usually began by pointing to fundamental similarities between all commercial organisations. Notwithstanding that, they were unanimous in their view that the industry is exceptional in a number of ways. Collectively, they provided me with a wealth of reasons why this belief was justified, from the high expectations our society places on the industry to the exquisite sophistication of the science they used, and from the enormous potential for harm their work involved to the intense concentration of brain-power that sat under the roofs of their companies.

This evidence for exceptionalism coalesced under analyses to four measures of the industry, as described in this chapter. Along each individual measure, the life sciences industry may not be wholly unique, but it does lie at the far end of the distribution for social impact, complexity, risk and workforce composition. And, just as a truly exceptional individual may not be unique in any single trait but unique in her or his combination of characteristics, so it is with the life sciences industry. No other industry is so far from typical along so many dimensions. The life sciences industry really is exceptional.

This is the first lesson that the industry's leaders have learned. They all recognise that their industry and their organisation is special not only in superficial detail but, because of the confluence of these four factors, at a fundamental level. They have also learned, implicitly or explicitly, the implications of this exceptionalness. Whatever leadership basics might apply to all industries, leadership in the life sciences must be different from – and tailored to – its exceptional context. This first lesson forms the basis for all the other lessons they have learned. The other lessons are the subject of the following chapters.

2 The mission matters

Do mission statements matter? These explicit, publicised expositions of a firm's reason to exist and its values became popular in the 1980s although, by then, the term had been around for four decades. Many firms across all industries now have a mission statement adorning their annual report and hanging in their reception area. But search for articles about them and you are much more likely to find discussions of their uselessness, fatuity and insincerity. These criticisms revolve around the issue that they don't work the way they are supposed to. They are supposed to engender employees' emotional commitment towards shared goals and values. But sceptics say that, in a world where the real goal is to make more money for investors who are already much richer than the employees, mission statements don't fool anyone. From the point of view of sceptical employees, mission statements are a not-very-sophisticated confidence trick to be humoured or mocked. The academic literature provides little or no evidence that mission statements make a significant difference to any measure of organisational performance.

However, this pervasive scepticism about the value of a collective mission does not seem to extend to the life sciences industry, even though life science firms are as focused on shareholder returns as any of their non-life science peers. On the contrary, the interviewees for this book described the mission as a genuinely useful and essential leadership methodology. As Jean-Christophe Tellier and many others made clear, alignment around a common goal is a very powerful motivator, and a leader's role is to provide vision and direction around that goal. Naturally, I probed for why pharma and medical technology companies should differ from most other, more sceptical businesses. What emerged was that the importance and usefulness of mission statements was an adaptation to the four exceptional features of the life sciences industry uncovered in Lesson 1.

The social contract demands a meaningful mission

The social contract that exists between the life sciences industry and the society in which it operates is unwritten, powerful and, from one perspective, disingenuous. Society encourages and enables the industry to make healthy profits from human suffering and discomfort, but it is not wholly comfortable with the idea. It would rather the industry be a beneficent not-for-profit, if it could be so whilst still delivering innovations that improve, extend and save lives. To reconcile the somewhat contradictory desire to be a benevolent profit seeker, society expects that life science companies balance their financial objectives with equally important humanitarian goals. When life science companies appear to put financial returns above patient needs, they are pilloried by the media, shunned by investors and eschewed by employees, as we have seen in a number of notorious price-hike cases. They must therefore demonstrate a commitment to a mission to improve patient lives in some way. Any life science company leader that did not formulate, promulgate and respect such a mission would be seen to be breaking the social contract and would not survive. Of course, some Life Science Leaders have been tempted to use a mission as an insincere, fake cover for profiteering, but society seems to be savvy enough to see through this. Many of the interviewees drew a clear line between these "financial engineers" and the genuinely mission-led companies. Gabriel Baertschi felt that, in his experience, all good CEOs in this industry are genuinely interested in the science and patient outcomes. It is, in his view, part of their personal value system and is quite different from those CEOs who are primarily interested in financial engineering. Jeremy Levin articulated the same belief in typically robust style when he said that, in some firms, "leadership BS" has contaminated the industry with top-line-driven financial engineering that is not really concerned with innovation or the patient.

It seems then that, even in the absence of other reasons, the exceptional, implicit contract that the life sciences industry has with society would push its leaders to genuinely and sincerely use mission statements in a way that is different from other industries. To return to my evolutionary comparison, the normative pressure created by the social contract element of the environment has selected in favour of mission-led companies and disfavoured those who do not have, or who fake, genuine and beneficent missions.

The complexity of the industry requires mission-guided discretion

If, as I argued in Lesson 1, the life sciences industry is exceptionally complex on both its demand and supply sides, then this has important implications for how its leaders lead. One aspect of this is discretion, or freedom to act. From a management science perspective, the tasks that leaders assign to managers and employees vary along a spectrum between discretionary and non-discretionary. The latter are tasks that can be tightly specified, closely directed, constantly monitored and their outcomes directly rewarded or sanctioned. By contrast, discretionary tasks are performed with a high degree of autonomy, towards outcomes that are qualitative or hard to measure and, therefore, difficult to directly reward or sanction. Although all jobs contain a mixture of discretionary and non-discretionary tasks, the proportion of the former tends to increase with the complexity of the situation and the level of expertise of the job holder.

In a complex life science company, staffed with a high proportion of experts, many roles necessarily have a high degree of discretion. This freedom to act has significant potential downsides. Autonomous employees can act, deliberately or otherwise, in ways that are counter to the firm's best interests or that run counter to its strategy. Importantly, business complexity and the independence of expert employees also means that tightly bureaucratic management control systems are unable to counter these unintended negative consequences of employee discretion. In this situation, a clearly expressed and defined mission acts as a set of guidelines within which discretion can operate safely. This makes leadership both more effective and less onerous. As Peter Stein expressed it, leadership is easier when you have a clear sense of mission. Using mission to guide discretionary activity also helps define the focus of the CEO's activity. As Michel Pettigrew revealed in my interview with him, an important part of his role is to keep people focused on the unmet medical need and on using science to meet that need.

So, in addition to the selection pressure of the social contract, a clearly articulated mission is necessary in the life sciences industry because of its complexity and its workforce of independently-minded experts. Because of these two factors, much work in the sector has a high discretionary content, which is inevitable but which carries risks. This autonomy and risk can't be tightly controlled by bureaucracy, so mission statements have evolved as a useful replacement for bureaucratic systems. CEOs have learned to set missions and use them, rather than spend their time attempting tight command and control.

Missions provide insurance against reputational risk

When Andy Thompson was interviewed, he spoke passionately about how he works in a high-trust network of stakeholders and how hard he and his colleagues have to work to build genuine trust, contrasting it sharply with "just PR". His sentiments were reflected by many of the other interviewees too, revealing the reality that, when a life science company goes to market, the assets at risk are as much reputational as financial. Success in this complex environment depends on maintaining the trust of patients, professionals, payers and collaboration partners as well as investors, employees and other stakeholders. And, in an environment where demonstrable, tangible success may take many years to provide, this precious asset of trust rests in large part on the subjective perception of those stakeholders. In particular, trust rests on perceptions that the life science company shares the aims and interests of its stakeholders. This trust is hard to build but, by contrast, relatively easily destroyed by unfortunate trial results, opaque pricing decisions, forced re-allocation of resources, poor communication or other events that undermine trust between the company and its stakeholders.

To counter this imbalance between hard-won and easily-lost reputation, firms need a clear and consistent narrative around which to structure their communication and relationship with stakeholders. As Roland Diggelmann opined, firms need a transparent and consistent narrative with their external stakeholders. Into this context, a clearly articulated mission emerges as a form of insurance against reputational risk. By providing a fixed point around which strategic decisions are made, the mission enables a consistent narrative that stresses how the firm's interests align to those of its external stakeholders. As Jean-Christophe reminded me, even when stakeholders have different proximate aims, they share the same ultimate aim. What stakeholder could differ, for example, with the mission that Gabriel Baertschi expounded for his firm, Grünenthal, to create a world without pain?

A strong mission statement not only signals compliance with the social contract and provides guidance to discretionary action by expert, autonomous employees, it also has an important role in mitigating reputational risk by maintaining the trust of stakeholders. It seems that Life Science Leaders have learned to repurpose mission statements, which were originally intended for internal audiences, to provide this additional and essential benefit.

Missions enable the affective commitment of experts

The workforce composition of life science companies, with highly expert people across the organisation and a very low proportion of low-skilled workers, is necessary for them to achieve their goals. But the other side of that coin is that such people cannot be recruited and retained, motivated and led in the same way as low-skilled workforces. They are attractive to other employers, and who they choose to work for and how hard they choose to work is a not an enforced choice or necessity. This makes their personal commitment of great importance to the effectiveness of the company. When it comes to commitment, academics differentiate between three different kinds. Continuance commitment is the kind that is bought by salary when someone needs to pay the bills. Normative commitment is the kind that keeps people in a job either because it is part of their social life or their social circle expects them to do that job. Affective commitment is that which arises from shared values and beliefs. Most employees' commitment to their work is an amalgam of all three types of commitment but the proportions tend to vary with employee type. In broad terms, low-skilled employees are driven largely by continuance and normative commitment whilst experts, who have more choice and whose financial security needs are more satisfied, are driven by affective commitment. In this context, a beneficent and humanitarian mission emerges as a way of building the affective commitment of expert workforces to the organisation. Deborah Dunsire articulated what many employees of life science companies must feel when she explained that, although she is a qualified medical doctor, she felt that working for her company had a multiplier effect, amplifying her ability to be a force for good in the world.

So, given an expert workforce, the ability of an appropriate and compelling mission to create affective commitment has unique value. It is the fourth factor in a quartet of reasons why mission statements are genuinely useful in the life sciences, even as they have fallen into disrepute and ridicule in other sectors. Life Science Leaders have learned, or perhaps intuited, the value of mission statements. But, to appreciate this better, it is also important to understand how they use them.

Mission statements as lodestars

I entered the research process for this book with a somewhat sceptical view of how leaders use mission statements. This view was formed by the pervasive tone of the literature in this area and, I admit, by my personal experience of seeing benevolent missions used as masks for profit orientation. So, I was surprised by the prominence and emphasis that Life Science Leaders gave to the role of a well-articulated mission. Kieran Murphy told me, in a tone that implied it was very obvious to him and should be to everyone, that everything his firm does starts with the question of why they exist, which is to work with the healthcare professionals to solve the patients' problems. Jeremy Levin said something very similar, answering his own rhetorical question about why his firm exists with the need to serve the customer. In fact, every interviewee said something similar, with the only minor differences stemming from the specific market context. The mission matters much more than I realised at the beginning of my research and it has this prominence in the life science sector, and not in others, because of the combined pressure of the four factors described above.

As is the way in all research, my first finding – the prominence of the mission – led to further questions. In my supplementary probing, I sought to uncover how Life Science Leaders make use of their articulated mission. This seemed important because it was clear that the statements had some practical use and were not simply decorative adornments for their office wall. What emerged were two complementary uses of statements of the organisational mission. Firstly, mission statements are used as a "first hurdle" for strategic choices to jump. Only strategic choices that contribute significantly to the mission are allowed to proceed to a more detailed assessment of feasibility. In this way, the mission statement acts as a brake on the passions of departments who have a great, but not necessarily mission-enhancing, idea. Allan Hillgrove described this as one of the roles of his leadership group, encouraging his people to step back from the detail and to take a bigger perspective on what the ambition of the company really is.

Secondly, mission statements are used as a way to create behavioural norms, the company-wide expectations about what is and what is not acceptable and desirable behaviour. Several interviewees talked about Volkswagen's engineers' development of a "defeat device" to outwit emissions testers. They cited this as an example of behaviour led by immediate, operational goals rather than by a beneficent mission and as something they would neither expect nor tolerate in a life science company. Russell Mably, for example, had genuine passion in his voice when he described how his firm's mission to serve the surgeon set the flavour and tone of their everyday working.

The mission really matters

That the mission matters is the second lesson that Life Science Leaders have learned. For them, mission statements are essential and useful tools. They are not platitudinous media-relations exercises, framed and hung in reception but, to quote Hamlet, more honoured in the breach than the observance. Like an anteater's tongue or a bat's echo-location, organisational missions are adaptations to the environment and they have real, practical uses. In particular, they are adaptations to the four defining characteristics of the life sciences industry described in Lesson 1 and they are used to focus strategy and to shape behavioural norms.

3   The big issue is bicongruence

What single issue is most important to all leaders in the life sciences industry? It's an important question because, if they all share the same fundamental challenge, then companies can learn from each other and knowledge from one company is transferable to another. But, if the main issue facing life science companies is always idiosyncratic, then each company must solve that issue using its own experience, and its development will be limited by that. For that reason, I wanted to understand if there was a single, shared issue. But my training told me that this was too wide a question to ask and that it was better to ask lots of indirect questions, hoping that a shared answer would emerge.

As I asked many, varied interview questions about how they led and what they had learned, I was trying to uncover whether there was one thing at the front of all their minds, despite the differences in their companies, market areas and technologies. To my delight, a clear issue did emerge. To my surprise, given that I was talking to people who ran companies at the leading edge of the life sciences, that issue was over 200 years old. And, since that issue is fundamental to how Life Science Leaders spend their time and focus their attention, allow me a paragraph or two to explain it before I describe how they address this, their most important, shared issue.

At the end of the 18th century, the industrial revolution led to the growth of huge "manufactories" that replaced the earlier, pre-industrial model of cottage workers toiling away independently in their family homes. This new model was much more efficient than the old, and the Scots economist Adam Smith set out to discover why. To greatly simplify his findings, he attributed the efficiency of factories to a combination of two factors: specialisation and coordination. The pin factory workers he studied became more efficient by concentrating on one part of the production process and nothing else. In doing so, they became highly efficient experts and wasted no time swapping between tasks. The factory owners tapped into that efficiency by coordinating the many different tasks involved in pin production. Every specialised worker produced the right amount of output at the right time so that neither time nor money was wasted. Smith's specialise-and-coordinate explanation of how complex organisations work has been the foundation of industrial economics ever since. To modern eyes, it is so obvious that we often forget it.

Two centuries after Adam Smith, British management scientists Gibson Burrell and Gareth Morgan looked again at specialisation and coordination, this time from a sociological perspective. They didn't refute Smith but they provided a deeper, more interesting interpretation of his work that was more suited to the modern era. Again, I am simplifying their findings when I say Burrell and Morgan realised two things. The first was that, in the modern, knowledge-based economy, being expert and specialised meant understanding and applying the latest knowledge in your particular field. Burrell and Morgan called this fit between specialists and their particular part of the outside world "macrocongruence" and they realised that this was a necessary but not sufficient condition for organisational effectiveness. In short, experts become valuable only if they are truly expert.

Burrell and Morgan's second observation was that, in a complex modern organisation with many diverse, specialist functions, coordination becomes more difficult. They realised that, as specialists specialise to maintain macrocongruence, coordination between them becomes harder. This is because the language and world view of specialists becomes more and more differentiated from those of their colleagues in other functions, who are also specialising to maintain macrocongruence with their own, different part of the outside world. Imagine, for example, how difficult it is for a world-class immunologist and a world-class health economist to cooperate. Burrell and Morgan called the coordination between specialists within an organisation "microcongruence" and they realised that, like macrocongruence, it was necessary but not sufficient to organisational effectiveness. In essence, their contribution to understanding organisational effectiveness was that organisations must be "bicongruent" (that is, simultaneously macro- and microcongruent) but that, as knowledge advances, specialists become more specialised and organisations become more complex, achieving bicongruence becomes ever harder.

As my interviewees talked, I realised that the issues that really concerned them were not the obvious challenges of intense competition, transformative technology or changing markets. As leaders, they seemed very confident of their organisation's ability to overcome almost any challenge. But that confidence was conditional on maintaining bicongruence. In particular, it was conditional on maintaining bicongruence even as an ever more technologically advanced environment and an increasingly complex organisation made sustaining bicongruence ever harder. As Stephen Moran cogently expressed it, life science companies bring together quite amazing networks of expert specialists but with their expertise comes their ability, if they so choose, to stop anything they don't agree with. Unsurprisingly, none of my interviewees used the word bicongruence. They talked a lot about coordination, fit and alignment between processes, functions and business units. But it was very clear that bicongruence was the focus of their attention. And, once I realised that, it became obvious that this focus on the very difficult problem of bicongruence was, yet again, an evolutionary adaptation to the four exceptional features of the industry discussed in Lesson 1, especially complexity and workforce composition. Whilst bicongruence is an issue in any advanced organisation, it is easier when the level of technical specialisation is relatively low and when competitiveness depends on relatively few areas of specialisation. But life science companies, with their extremes of knowledge intensity across a large number of specialisations, have necessarily created the conditions that make it exceptionally hard to achieve and maintain bicongruence. And, just as in biological evolution, when an especially difficult adaptation is fundamental to survival, it becomes what separates survival from extinction.

If achieving and maintaining bicongruence is the existential question facing Life Science Leaders, then how do they answer it? What are the levers they pull to coordinate a complex organisation of many different kinds of experts? This was the focus of my supplementary questions in this area and, as before, the conversations yielded a flood of individual responses that, on analysis, eventually resolved into three distinct but complementary answers. The answers concerned expectations of the leadership team, processes within it and trust between its members. They describe what happens inside the leadership team, where functional-expert leaders meet, with the aim of achieving and maintaining bicongruence.

Selecting and leading for organisational salience

It is axiomatic that senior leadership roles involve difficult choices between competing priorities and trade-offs against conflicting demands. Management scientists who study this observe that one of the most important factors to shape such choices is the balance between group and organisational salience. By this, they mean the priority, in terms of interest and allegiance, that executives give to the sub-unit they represent (i.e. group salience) versus that given to the organisation as a whole (i.e. organisational salience). Group salience, that is allegiance to a department or team, tends to predominate at middle and lower levels of management. To some extent, it is encouraged by organisational systems. For example, individual targets often recognise functional outcomes, such as meeting sales targets, rather than organisational aims, such as profit or return on investment. Group salience is often seen as a way to improve normative commitment (see Lesson 2 and how missions enable the affective commitment of experts), which is the aim of team-building exercises. Group salience may have benefits, such as when medical and technical staff feel a duty to professional standards that might otherwise be threatened by commercial expediency. But at higher levels in the organisation, group salience becomes counterproductive. It leads to cognitive biases when complex problems are seen through a distorted, functional lens. It can also lead to misalignment of goals as executives bias their efforts to achieve group, rather than organisational, aims. Worst of all, group salience is often implicit and disguised by executives claiming to put the interests of the company first.

Life Science Leaders have learned two things about group and organisational salience. The first is that group salience within the leadership team is especially destructive in the context of a very complex organisation full of specialised experts. This is because, in a less specialised context where peers understand something of their colleagues' fields, peers are more able to challenge each other. However, in a more specialised context where peers can have only superficial understanding of each other's fields, challenging is harder and obstruction is easier, thus embedding and exacerbating group-salient behaviour. The second lesson is that functional leaders, when elevated to the leadership team, vary in their ability to replace their group salient behaviour with organisationally salient behaviour. As Louise Makin explained, members of her leadership team have functional responsibility, but they must not be "Members of Parliament", who only represent a functional or professional constituency. Will McGuire made a very similar point when he described how he expected his leadership team to represent their department but make decisions for their company. As a result of these lessons, Life Science Leaders encourage and expect organisationally salient behaviour in their leadership teams. This rare, valuable ability to behave in an organisationally salient way whilst still leading a specialised function becomes an essential criterion for entry to the leadership team and group salient behaviour is discouraged or punished.

Selecting and managing the leadership team for their organisational salience seems to emerge as the first step in achieving bicongruence in life science companies. It may be useful in other industries too, of course, but in life sciences the need for a high degree of organisational salience is intensified to an exceptional degree because, in a complex organisation with a leadership team of highly expert peers, other approaches to aligning the senior team, such as a very assertive CEO or intra-team negotiation, are much less effective.

Delegating macrocongruence and focusing on microcongruence

It is obviously essential that each function and process within a life science company must understand and fit with its particular external environment. Regulatory departments could not be effective without alignment to the demands of regulatory bodies; new product development must be attuned to the latest relevant technology; marketing processes must reflect customer decision-making processes and so on. But these matters of macrocongruence are largely delegated by Life Science Leaders. According to Roland Diggelmann, technical competence within their own specialised area is assumed for leadership team members and the focus is on their contribution to the team. When asked, almost all the interviewees made clear that ensuring macrocongruence (although they did not used that specialised term) was a matter for functional leaders.

Instead, leaders in this industry concentrate their efforts on how to achieve microcongruence – coordination between functions – in the context of a team of experts whose subject complexity and knowledge intensity makes coordination difficult. For example, Kieran Murphy pointed to the need to be very diligent in ensuring that nothing went wrong at the connections between one process or department and another. In his comments and others like it, I heard again the evolutionary adaptation of the life sciences industry to the selection pressures created by the four exceptional characteristics described in Lesson 1. The social contract, technical complexity, high risks and expert workforces all select against leadership teams that took an ad hoc, informal approach to achieving microcongruence. Equally, those four factors select for more rigorous processes for coordination within the leadership team. Given its obvious importance, I probed further to understand what they had learned about achieving microcongruence. Consistent with their different businesses and personalities, the interviews revealed many differences of detail in how Life Science Leaders manage their leadership teams, but three common sub-routines did emerge.

The first was, as far as a possible, to isolate the team from immediate time pressures. Peter Stein stressed the importance of allowing enough time for discussion so that critical interdependencies were not missed. The second sub-routine was that of forcing problems and ideas into the open, so that nothing important was left unsaid. Andy Thompson described his variant of that approach as a "disagree and commit" routine in which problems are broken down, then a diversity of ideas was generated before the team focused on solutions. As numerous interviewees mentioned, this approach seems necessary in order to both avoid orthodox thinking and to challenge unwarranted assumptions. The third idea was procedural: issues that were too large and complex to be handled effectively by the leadership team were broken down and delegated to subgroups. Meinrad Lugan, for example, described his method of splitting difficult questions across multiple specialist groups with some overlap, which eventually fed their conclusions back into the leadership team.

In these sub-routines, we can see two lessons that Life Science Leaders have learned about how to address their most important issue, which is bicongruence. The first is to delegate macrocongruence and assume its achievement by well-qualified, specialist members of the leadership team. This allows CEOs to concentrate on achieving the other component of bicongruence, microcongruence, which is especially difficult in the context of a complex company with a highly expert workforce. The second lesson is that achieving microcongruence requires very specific attention; techniques like allocating time, breaking down the issue and splitting its solution into pieces all make sense from a microcongruence perspective. Together, these routines can be seen as part of an adaption to the problem of achieving bicongruence, something that is existentially important in the life sciences industry.

Maintaining a foundation of trust

As I describe above, a focus on organisational over group salience, and processes for enabling microcongruence were clearly factors of which my interviewees were very conscious. Those two factors, although described using different words and without the academic framework that I take from Burrell and Morgan, are clearly central to enabling any leadership team to do the difficult job of achieving and maintaining bicongruence in a complex organisation of experts. But, as I listened, I recognised there was an elephant in the room, something that was important but implicit and unspoken. This only emerged later in the interviews, as the interviewees opened up somewhat. It was the matter of trust.

Trust is a slippery concept, one of those words that means different things to different people in different situations. To management scientists, it means the belief, held by people in a business relationship, that the other parties in that relationship will not act, or fail to act, in such a way as to damage the interests of the counterparties. Trust plays a limited role in very transactional relationships, where what each party must deliver is tangible, performance is transparent and interaction short-lived. Where trust becomes critically important is in situations of uncertainty, ambiguity or opacity, when one's colleagues could damage one's interests without being obviously culpable or facing the consequences and when relationships must endure.

This technical, precise definition of trust as a belief is relevant in the context of life science leadership because the complexity of the business creates exceptional degrees of uncertainty, ambiguity and opacity and the leadership team requires a level of stability. In this context, every member of a leadership team has the potential to actively or passively damage the interests of one or more colleagues without being seen to do so. Failing to reveal information, allowing colleagues to make mistakes and withholding support are all very easy in a context where your colleagues can't possibly know and understand more than a fraction of what you are doing. In the jargon of this field, leadership teams require a high level of mutual trust.

After selecting and leading for organisational salience, assuming macrocongruence and managing for microcongruence, it emerged that, in order to achieve and maintain bicongruence, Life Science Leaders pull the mutual trust "lever". How they work that lever is not entirely clear; it is obviously a very emotional, implicit process. Some, like Jean-Christophe Tellier talked of trust as arising from shared purpose. Others, like Will McGuire, saw personal honesty and integrity as the antecedents of trust. Peter Martin stressed the value of continuity of a small leadership team, which encouraged apolitical behaviour. Unlike other areas of my questioning, there was not a clear, non-obvious consensus about how to create trust. I formed the opinion that trust probably arose from a combination of shared purpose, integrity and close co-working. It seems clear that trust is indeed a sort of lubricant for the leadership team, but much less obvious how it is created. The ability to create and maintain trust is probably tacit knowledge that leaders have, like riding a bike, that is hard to communicate. Lack of trust was universally seen as a critical failure that would cripple a team, but the mechanics of trust-creation are unfathomable and how exactly it influences the working of the leadership team remains nebulous. In as much as there is a single source from which trust flows, it seems to lie somewhere in the individual humanity of the CEO, as discussed in Lesson 5.

Bicongruence: A function of salience, process and trust

This is the third lesson that Life Science Leaders have learned. Bicongruence, in Burrell and Morgan's terminology, is necessary and important to any organisation. But, as Mark Twain said of civilisations, it contains the seeds of its own destruction. Macrocongruence with the external environment is as essential as microcongruence with the internal environment. But the former makes the latter harder, and vice versa. This is especially true in the life sciences industry, where macrocongruence demands exceptional levels of specialisation and microcongruence must be achieved between many diverse specialisms. It is clear that bicongruence is forged in the leadership team.

Indeed, it can be argued that bicongruence is the function of the leadership team. Life Science Leaders have learned that it has three prerequisites, so they select their team for organisational salience, they use processes that find and fix the most difficult points of alignment between functions and then they lubricate the whole process with trust, which is as essential as it is enigmatic.

4 The leader is a Decisive Facilitator

What role does the Life Science Leader take in the leadership team? It's an important question because, if there is a template then, like all templates, it can guide and accelerate the learning of new leaders. If, on the other hand, each leader creates her or his own personality-specific role then learning to lead is harder, but at least we can caution against using inappropriate templates. The management science literature, and still more the shelves of airport bookshops, is awash with different models and styles of leadership. My own LinkedIn feed is infested with trite memes: photographs of Steve Jobs, Elon Musk or Richard Branson with glib quotes telling me about what good leaders do and don't do. Look carefully, and these commonplace ideas about leadership are obviously polarised and contradictory. On the one hand, we lionise visionary heroes like Steve Jobs, implying that leaders should be strong, decisive and perhaps a little asocial. On the other, there is a social expectation that our leaders ought to be humble servants who are privileged to do no more than enable the real heroes, their workforce. This is at least what Richard Branson's media relations would have us believe. The importance of the question and the conflicting views on the literature made this a focus of my interviews.

Neither of the dichotomised hero or servant models rings true in my long experience of the life sciences industry and nor do they bear much resemblance to the interviewees for this book. Evolutionary theory says that we shouldn't expect them to because if, as I discussed in Lesson 1, the life sciences industry is exceptional then we should not expect its leaders' styles to conform to these stereotypes, which don't consider industry specificities. Instead, evolutionary ideas should guide us to hypothesise that leaders should adapt to the four industry-specific conditions discussed in Lesson 1, resulting in a style that is neither hero nor servant but something quite characteristic of the industry. Testing that hypothesis and uncovering the role that Life Science Leaders took in their leadership team was an important part of my interview questioning. What emerged was not only a test of the evolutionary hypothesis but also some key lessons about how Life Science Leaders play their role effectively.

The Decisive Facilitator adaptation

By the time my interviews reached the questions about how leaders lead, we had already discussed what made the industry special. So, the context of the interviewees' answers was that the industry was exceptional and the interviewees described how they had developed behaviours that fitted with the particular context of the industry. The interviewees' answers made clear that the sort of hero or servant leadership styles described in airport books and magazine articles were not good descriptions of how they themselves behaved.

The industry's social contract, for example, does not favour hero leaders who single-handedly develop and champion a vision of the future. Unlike in other markets, the social mission of the life sciences industry creates a societal expectation of shared responsibility that is taken very seriously. As Will McGuire explained to me, an industry that can save, extend, improve or end lives is fantastically rewarding, but also places an enormous and palpable weight of responsibility on its leadership team. Equally, the complexity of the industry, on both supply and demand sides, is so beyond the comprehension of a single person, that it strongly disfavours autocratic leadership.

Maurits Wolleswinkel was unequivocal about this when he said that it was simply not possible for any one person to be an expert in every area of this complex business, a fact that implies that the best you can do is to understand enough to connect with the experts in the team. The magnitude and longevity of risk in the industry also selects against charismatic individualists. Yukio Matsui described his leadership team as mitigators and managers of both commercial and technical risk, a role that required an orchestra of expertise rather than a talented prima donna. And of course, since the composition of a life science company's leadership team reflects that of the overall workforce, these teams are usually exceptionally highly qualified and expert and are driven by affective commitment (see Lesson 2 and how missions enable the affective commitment of experts). As Kieran Murphy said, reflecting the view all of the interviewees, you can't simply tell these people what to do. In other words, all four selection pressures would work against any "Steve Jobs" of the life sciences industry. This seems a possible explanation for the demise, for example, of Elizabeth Holmes of Theranos.

The exceptional conditions of the industry disfavour servant leadership as much as heroes. Servant leadership styles are characterised by allowing a high degree of discretion to sub-ordinates. But, as we have seen in Lesson 3, the complex interrelatedness of the industry's expertise amplifies the challenge of bicongruence, and this does not fit well with the uncoordinated freedom to act that is implicit in servant leadership. Equally, the magnitude and longevity of the risks that characterise the sector also makes it unrealistic to allow a high degree of independent activity. And both the social contract and the expert workforce place a high value on sharing expertise across functions, which is not a strong feature of servant leadership. In other words, servant leadership styles are as disfavoured by the industry's characteristics as are hero styles.

That is not to say that neither style has anything to offer the sector. As Deborah Dunsire explained to me, coordination of activity is made more difficult by specialisation, but it is the leader's job to make sure the team adds up to more than the sum of its parts. There are, undoubtedly, similarities between servant styles of leadership and what might be called facilitative leadership, but they are not identical. The latter provides a stronger direction towards goals than the former, even though both eschew micromanaging. Equally, some of the direction provided by hero-style leaders is obviously necessary, but direction and dictation are not the same thing.

It was clear then that neither of the currently popular stereotypes of leadership were realistic descriptions of what my interviewees do in the real world. So, if neither a hero nor a servant, what role does the Life Science Leader play in the leadership team? What emerged from the analysis here was one of the most clear-cut, unambiguous answers in all of the research. Life Science Leaders are best described as Decisive Facilitators. Will McGuire, using a figure of speech that was also used by other interviewees, said that he often felt like "the dumbest person in the room" and that, in that situation, it was impossible for him to provide technical insight; his role was to provide vision, culture and processes for the experts to do their job. Andy Thompson said something similar, describing his role as creating both the space to let others work and the focus around which to work. In the same vein, Michel Pettigrew described his role as synthesising the expertise of his team. In this way, all of the interviewees displayed a facilitative style. But all of the interviewees also made clear that, in addition to facilitating their expert team towards a decision, they also had the role of crystallising, resolving and manifesting that decision so that it translated to action. Without that role, there is a possibility that the conditions of complexity and high risk predispose the team to perpetual analysis and inaction. As I listened to the interviewees describe the decision-crystallisation part of their role, I was reminded of my school chemistry lessons. I would drop a single crystal of copper sulphate into a supersaturated solution and watch the solute suddenly fall out of solution and settle in the bottom of the beaker. The single, decisive crystal helps the solution over a thermodynamic energy "hump" which would otherwise prevent crystallisation. My interviewees' role was, I felt, to prepare the solution but also to force the crystallisation by helping the leadership team over the decision hump.

Being a Decisive Facilitator

So, there does appear to be a template for the role that Life Science Leaders play in the leadership team and one that is a reasonable description of all my interviewees. It is a template that is best described as a Decisive Facilitator. In research, however, every answer creates more questions. If Life Science Leaders are Decisive Facilitators, how do they do that? What lessons have they learned about how to play this role in practice? My supplementary questions pushed in this direction and, as with my other questions, a blizzard of individual answers swept over me. These resolved, during later analysis, into a small number of common themes. These seem to follow a chronological pattern, describing a series of five key steps of the Decisive Facilitator as she or he shepherds the leadership team towards strategic choices.

Step 1: Defining decision scope

Both in my research interviews and in my advisory work with life science companies, I am often privy to the details of the questions facing leadership teams. These are rarely well defined, binary questions for which the data is plentiful and clear. Frequently, they are what knowledge management scientists call "wicked problems", problems resistant to resolution due to their complexity and changing parameters. A team of lesser talents might be paralysed by wicked problems, but that of a typical life science company is full to bursting with expertise and perhaps a little hubris. Faced with wicked problems, these leadership teams of experts suffer from an embarrassment of riches with respect to ideas and opinions. Interviewees often spoke of there being no shortage of suggestions and no lack of enthusiasm in the leadership team. Instead, the danger lies in going "off piste" or "tilting at windmills" or "giving a great answer to the wrong question", to use some of the phrases used by my interviewees. This itinerant tendency is a by-product of the diverse professional cultures and world views in most life science leadership teams. Even with broad-based knowledge acquired from experience, the perspectives of, for example, commercial, financial and scientific people are often shaped by their professional training and the sub-culture of their profession, leading them to come at the same problem from very different angles. This diversity and fecundity of approaches has its merits, but it also threatens sub-optimal decisions.

Because of this tendency towards a diversity of approaches, Life Science Leaders saw their first job as corralling their team's thinking and steering it towards the issues at hand. Andy Thompson described setting the vision and purpose and getting out of the way. More graphically, Roland Diggelmann talked of how he painted the lines of the tennis court, prescribing where the team had to play but not how. In this, we see a particular method of using the mission, as discussed in Lesson 2, to direct and motivate the most senior and expert part of an expert workforce. It lies somewhere in between the "envision and dictate" style characteristic of autocratic leaders and the "create the environment and allow free rein" approach espoused by the servant school of leadership. Again, it is best understood as an adaptation to the four exceptional characteristics of the industry discussed in Lesson 1. Given those four conditions, the Life Science Leader must begin, guided by the mission, with defining the scope of the decisions to be made.

Being a Decisive Facilitator, then, begins with deciding on where the lines on the tennis court are painted; the parameters and context of any decision. Without that decision, the "wickedness" of the problems provoke the managerial equivalent of a "cytokine storm" and this wealth of perspectives, knowledge and ideas can hinder rather than help the decision process. The first step in decisive facilitation is to avoid such a storm.

Step 2: Creating the human systems

Always, the most interesting and exciting findings in my research are those that don't fit in with my preconceptions. I had begun my interviews with an implicit assumption that leadership teams made decisions in traditional group format, with everyone contributing an opinion until a decision was made. But what emerged from the research was that a significant part of the leaders' role is to set up and use alternatives to this approach. Andy Thompson called this the setting up of "human systems", choosing the modes of interaction between the experts that allows their expertise to be synthesised. Interviewees described a variety of such systems. Meinrad Lugan described how he, or some sub-group of experts, created prototype solutions and invited criticism as a means of solving difficult issues. Deborah Dunsire talked of her technique of separating the debate from the decision. Russell Mably described his company's habits of always pulling discussions back to the facts and data. Other interviewees stressed the cultural and behavioural norms that complemented these techniques for decision making. Andy Thompson talked about creating a "cultural bias for action", whilst Russell Mably emphasised the importance of avoiding the discussion becoming personal, which is easy to do in a context of strongly held beliefs and commitment to the best outcomes. This combination of techniques for addressing questions and their complementary culturally embedded behaviours together constitute "human systems" and their design is an important part of the Life Science Leader's role.

It seems that, after deciding on the parameters of a decision, decisive facilitation relies on the establishment of a "modus operandi" for the leadership team. Without that, it is hard to synthesise the expertise around the table and too easy for it to descend into interpersonal conflict.

Step 3: Avoid critical information gaps

By this point in the analysis of the interviews, I could see that defining the scope of any decision and setting up the human systems for addressing them were lessons that all of my interviewees had learned. In doing these two things, Life Science Leaders created the machinery by which the leadership team functioned. But a machine needs the right inputs to work on and the next finding to emerge from the analysis concerned what Life Science Leaders had learned about that. Again, it can be best understood as an adaptation to the exceptional characteristics of the industry: when an expert team addresses a very complex situation the risk is not that they won't have the intellectual capacity to solve it. The most likely cause of a weak decision flows from missing something critical, in oversimplifying an issue or in not understanding the various tensions and contradictions that are inherent in wicked problems. In other words, the challenge lies in giving the team the right information to work with.

With this in mind, the interviewees all talked about the time and effort they put into "surfacing" or "making clear" the factors involved in a decision *before* they attempted to decide anything. As they described this, the picture in my mind was of a chef, gathering together bowls of prepared ingredients before she or he begins cooking. Interviewees spoke of this stage with an unusual fervour. Allan Hillgrove was passionate about the need to engage strongly with his team so that the richness of the situation, not just the superficialities, came out. Gabriel Baertschi was equally fervent in stressing the need to identify and weigh all of the factors relevant to a discussion. Maurits Wolleswinkel talked of the value of thinking in the abstract so that he could step back from the details and identify gaps in the information being presented. Meinrad Lugan underlined how important it was to hear everyone's voice, not just the most relevant to the topic, to ensure that a decision was made with the fullest possible information. Not only was this issue-surfacing activity emphasised by all of the interviewees, they also shared a tone that implied they had all, at some stage, had the experience of missing or neglecting some important factor that had later come back to haunt them.

The third critical element of decisive facilitation, then, is to ensure that the decision is based on the fullest possible information. This is again an adaptation to complexity in the industry that makes it hard to identify all the necessary information, and to the magnitude of the risk, which amplifies the consequences of poorly informed decisions. Laxity at this stage would render even the most effective human systems, working on a perfectly-defined issue, ineffective.

Step 4: Maximising integrative conflict

Given the wicked nature of the problems faced and a leadership team of diverse expertise and world views, it would be odd if there were not some conflict within the leadership team. Conflict, to a management scientist, has two facets. We refer to both distributive and integrative conflict. Distributive conflict is negative and characterised by individuals or functions working against each other by using guerrilla tactics, such as withholding information or working strict interpretations of roles. Integrative conflict is positive and is characterised by constructive challenges, sharing of resources and role flexibility. According to research in this area, effective teams are characterised not by lack of conflict, but by a high ratio of integrative over distributive conflict.

I trod softly when my questioning probed for evidence of conflict. It is often something that executives prefer not to talk about. But in this case, I was impressed to hear most of the executives describe not only the reality of conflict but also its value. In particular, their responses revealed how they do not try to suppress conflict within the leadership team but instead strive to maximise the integrative/distributive ratio, just as the prior research implied they should. Lars Fruergaard Jørgensen pointed to the value of tensions in the team as a way of improving decisions. Jane Griffiths and Gabriel Baertschi said much the same, with the emphasis on managing conflict for its positive outcomes. Deborah Dunsire illuminated part of the mechanism of integrative conflict when she indicated its value in getting all of the expert players to raise their game. Many of the interviewees described the fundamentals of behaviour that led to a good integrative/distributive conflict ratio: mutual respect, shared vision and clear, transparent processes for using information. Louise Makin emphasised the value of everyone knowing their role, which was interesting to hear because fuzzy role boundaries are one of the factors that research identifies as a cause of distributive conflict.

Managing to achieve integrative rather than distributive conflict is the fourth step in how Life Science Leaders enact their Decisive Facilitator role. Given the nature of the team and the wicked problems, conflict is inevitable; but the right kind of conflict may also be essential. The appropriate ratio seems to enable effective human systems, working with full information, to address well-defined questions.

Step 5: Precipitating the decision

The final stage in how Life Science Leaders enact the Decisive Facilitator role was perhaps hardest to uncover. Patrice Baudry was typical of all of the interviewees when he stressed that leadership decisions were usually consensual and hardly ever made by the CEO in the absence of consensus. Some attributed consensus to the "scientific" culture of the industry, whilst others perceived it to be a facet of national cultures. Despite these claims, my interviewees' descriptions of how they worked suggested that life science leadership teams act to avoid the indecision sometimes associated with very consensual decision-making processes.

Notwithstanding claims of consensual decision making, it was clear that the Life Science Leaders I spoke to took steps to force the decision to emerge from the consensus, to "crystallise" or "gel" the different perspectives. These were just some of the expressions I wrote in my notes. In this, it seems that the role of Decisive Facilitator is to make the need for a choice clear. As in the examples already used, some leaders proposed prototype decisions to force challenge. Others made clear that inaction was not an option. Still others "threatened" to make a choice unilaterally if necessary. In all cases, I formed the opinion that Life Science Leaders generally did not simply assess the view of the majority and then decide based on that. More often, they did something that caused their leadership team to agree on a joint decision. It may seem like a subtle difference, but it appears to be an important one.

From setting a framework for decisions to establishing human systems and from surfacing issues to managing conflict, Life Science Leaders appear to move through a series of steps that not only facilitates their leadership team but also causes their shared decision to form. In doing so, they act neither as heroes nor as servants. Decisive Facilitators is the most accurate label to give this behaviour.

Decisive facilitation as a necessary adaptation

What role to play in a diversely expert leadership team is the fourth lesson that Life Science Leaders have learned. Neither heroic individualism nor privileged servitude describes accurately what they have learned to do because, to use a biologist's term, both of these styles would be maladaptive to the peculiarities of the industry's environment. Instead, Life Science Leaders have developed a leadership style that both focuses and facilitates the knowledge-intensive expertise of their teams, whilst at the same time pushing them to crystallise their decisions. The unanimity of their responses suggests that, whilst they may colour this style with their personal habits, no other leadership style would fit this industry environment.

5 Leadership is an intensely individualistic task

How much of leadership in the life sciences industry is procedural and systematic? It is an important question because procedural and systematic processes can be reduced to standardised processes, which are efficient, reproducible and mechanical. Much of the efficiency and effectiveness of modern business organisations is built on taking what were individualistic crafts and turning them into consistent, unvarying procedures that require less skill and produce satisfactory outcomes at a relatively low cost. This is true not only of manual tasks but also of so-called knowledge work. Just think how your firm creates a contract, a brand strategy or a regulatory submission. Boilerplate text, templates and checklists abound in all organisations. Mechanisable tasks can also be copied more easily, meaning that they very quickly become very similar in all firms and cease to be sources of competitive advantage. By contrast, those activities that are not procedural and systematic cannot be reduced to routine procedures; they remain personal, idiosyncratic and characteristic of the firm. Performed well, these distinctive activities can be a source of sustainable advantage. Performed badly, they can be a cause of competitive weakness. And because of this potential impact on competitiveness, it would be both interesting and useful to know whether the leadership of a life science company is a mechanistic task or a human, individualistic one.

The existing writing on leadership, especially those books that sell well, imply that leadership is somewhere towards the mechanical end of the spectrum. It is usually normative, meaning that it says or implies that there is a way that leaders ought to lead. This is even true of the literature that praises individual, "hero"-style leaders. Read a number of these books and a picture emerges of a strong-jawed, visionary, hard-nosed workaholic who somehow manages to inspire her or his followers and scare them at the same time. Even texts on so-called situational leadership, which counsel adapting leadership style to the circumstances, recommend a small pallet of fixed approaches to leadership. They say how leaders ought to behave in a limited number of contexts.

As my research interviews and analysis progressed, I became more and more curious about this question. Obviously, there would be variations in the detail of leaders' jobs; their businesses ranged from in vitro diagnostics to implants to medicines in every possible therapy area. But the exceptional characteristics of the industry also seemed to militate against any normative leadership style. A complex industry, with so much variation amongst its highly qualified workforce and a commitment to a social mission, did not seem consistent with any of the normative recommendations. So, my questions probed into how Life Science Leaders actually deal with their employees, not only their role in the leadership team (which I've discussed in Lesson 4) but also when they interact with people more generally.

The short answer to my question was that, far from being mechanistic, leadership in life science companies is intensely humanistic, based both on the individuality of the leader and that of the people she or he leads. I reached that conclusion because my analyses uncovered three components of leadership in the life sciences, each of which points towards individuality and away from a mechanistic approach. The first concerned the diversity of their employees, the second the importance of coaching and the third the need to act as a leader.

Making lemonade from cognitive diversity

All of the leaders interviewed spoke about the enormous variation of the personalities in their organisation. Sometimes this was framed in terms of functional stereotypes, such as geeky scientists, inflexible lawyers or ostentatious sales people. Often, it was expressed in terms of admiration of how individuals could generate and execute amazing, unexpected ideas or perform beyond expectations. Rarely, they spoke in frustration about embedded behaviours that limited performance. But the common theme was the huge heterogeneity of personality types and behaviours within their company. Jane Griffiths, whose love of people was evident in everything she said, stressed how her organisation was very diverse not just in the conventional sense of the term, meaning gender, age or ethnicity, but also in terms of cognitive and behavioural styles. It is essential, she said, for leadership to work with and make use of that diversity. Similarly, Louise Makin emphasised the need to accommodate those who, in my questioning, I had called mavericks. Namal Nawana talked about the need to encourage, rather than discourage, employees to express their compassion. Overall, the consensus view among the interviewees was that they had learned to treat cognitive and personality diversity as an asset to leverage, not a problem to fix. To use an idiom without any disrespect, when given lemons, Life Science Leaders choose to make lemonade.

When I pushed further to uncover what my interviewees had learned about leveraging cognitive diversity, two fascinating themes emerged. Firstly, attempts to change employees' fundamental personality attributes are of little use. Maurits Wolleswinkel emphasised that personality type cannot be right or wrong, it can only fit or not fit with the role and the team. Kieran Murphy gave a very clear explication of this when he talked about roles, such as in product development, that require a great deal of discipline in how work is done. In his view, personal attributes such as attention to detail and rigour of thinking are innate human qualities that can be developed to an extent but not implanted or taught. Secondly, the interviewees talked a lot about organisational culture as a vessel for containing, directing and exploiting cognitive diversity. Jean-Christophe Tellier told me that the culture the CEO creates is, in his view, the essence of performance. Jeremy Levin saw creation of the culture and acceptance of it by employees as the foundation of leadership. Life Science Leaders also see themselves as being responsible for cultural change. Lars Fruergaard Jørgensen described how he did this by openly articulating new assumptions, in his case about radical innovation. In similar tone, Allan Hillgrove was a strong believer in the need for leadership to communicate cultural values by being role models.

This part of my research told me that leadership in the life sciences industry cannot be mechanistic, in part because the workforce is so cognitively diverse. Leaders have learned that this diversity is an asset to be exploited and not changed, even if it could be. They have also learned that human diversity is best used within the framework of a clear culture, which they themselves must create, model and, when necessary, change.

Coaching as a leadership technique

One of the strongest, most consistent themes to come out of the interview analysis was the reference the Life Science Leaders made to coaching. Like many other words in the management lexicon, coaching is often used loosely with variable, unclear meanings, so I probed to understand what the interviewees meant by it. What they described was a very personal, individual process. Michel Pettigrew was typical when he told me how he began by asking people what they are not good at, as a means of understanding both their strengths and weaknesses. Russell Mably shared with me the lessons he had learned about the importance of empathy and of understanding what was going on in the other person's head. Maurits Wolleswinkel was especially eloquent when he discussed coaching. He wanted me to understand that there was no single coaching process and that it was a very situation-specific practice. Yukio Matsui, giving a specific example of coaching his colleagues to be more accessible to their own subordinates, praised the value of a well-coached employee. It is hard to argue with his view that bright people, given direction and coaching, need little managing and tend to motivate themselves. What we see in these responses is that coaching has a very specific meaning for Life Science Leaders and it is distinct from other leadership activity. It is a highly personal, very situation-specific process of enabling the individual to grow. It is quite different from giving directions about how to achieve a task. It requires patience, listening skills and empathy. It is, in other words, a very individualistic, human activity.

So, the importance of coaching as a technique of leadership in the life sciences reinforces the importance of making an asset of cognitive diversity. If such an important component of the leadership role is intrinsically centred around colleagues' needs and relies on the coach's personal skills, it is further evidence that leadership in the life sciences is an intensely individualistic task that could not be reduced to a standardised process. The importance of coaching can also be seen as an example of adaptation to the specific conditions of the industry, especially its complexity and the composition of its workforce. Coaching seems to be an adaptation for enabling experts to use their expertise.

Self-centred leadership

Qualitative researchers are trained to listen for the moment when an interviewee says something that is so unexpected, so dissonant to the interviewer's ideas, that it leads to a rich seam of questions and answers that were not in the original interview guide. This occurred early in my research for this book, when one interviewee described her style of leadership as self-centred. Since self-centred usually implies improper selfishness or inappropriate self-absorption, this was so surprising that I had to ask further questions and to alter my questioning in later interviews. What emerged from this additional course of discussion was that Life Science Leaders see their leadership behaviour as self-centred in the sense that it derives from their own personality and values. The interviewees almost all expressed a strong view that it was impossible to lead in a style that is not consistent with one's personality. Leadership, they argued, can't be faked. As Kieran Murphy put it, if you try to be someone else you will soon be found out. People follow people, as Louise Makin put it. This basic view led me to ask more questions about how their personalities influenced how they led. From the answers to these questions, three more lessons emerged.

The first was the value of self-knowledge, in the sense of understanding and adhering to one's own values. Each individual expressed this same idea in different words. Jeremy Levin spoke of the need to draw energy from one's personal philosophy. Yukio Matsui's view was that he would be unable to continue doing his job if he were unable to adhere to his personal values, especially with respect to honesty and integrity. That theme came out repeatedly. Deborah Dunsire saw the confidence that is required of her as having its origins in thoughtful, careful decisions that were consistent with her personal values. As I listened to the interviewees, I was reminded of the many philosophers who have expounded the importance of self-knowledge. As Adam Smith said, the first thing to know is yourself.

The second lesson that flowed from my questions about self-centred leadership was that, despite the variation in the styles and personalities of the interviewees, a small set of fundamental shared values and behaviours was shared by all of them. Three of these were most consistently cited. First, approachability. Andy Thompson described how occupying the leaders' role sometimes created, in the eyes of those he led, false perceptions of aloofness, and that he tried to break down this perception, whilst still maintaining authority. Russell Mably said something very similar when he described approachability as prerequisite for leading. The second, humility, was described in various ways, typified by Allan Hillgrove's assertion that a leader must be able to set her or his own ego to one side in order to effectively engage with others. Kieran Murphy showed both the wisdom of his vast experience and his Irish charm when he told me how confidence, paradoxically, comes from self-awareness, humility and not taking oneself too seriously. The last was emotional control, epitomised by Michel Pettigrew who spoke of the need to control emotions, especially with respect to issues in which he was emotionally invested. Maurits Wolleswinkel talked of the need for detachment and the risk of being too reflective, too close to human emotions.

Following on from self-knowledge and the common behaviours of approachability, humility and emotional control, there emerged a third and final consequence of leadership's foundations in the personality of the leader. This was the duty they felt to fulfil their obligations as leader. The interviewees spoke of bearing the responsibility of being *the* leader, using the definite article, and what that meant. For all that the role requires making use of the asset of cognitively diverse experts, for all that it involves coaching others to develop their talents and for all that it demands humility and controlled emotions, organisations need clear leadership. To leave a leadership gap was seen as not only damaging to the organisation, it was felt to be a neglect of their duty to colleagues and company. Lars Fruergaard Jørgensen put it forcefully and eloquently. A leader, he told me, needs to rise above others in the face of significant change, to articulate a new vision and to ignite the change. His words captured what many of the other interviewees said in different ways – that even complex organisations filled with experts need an individual they all can look to as the leader.

The human, individual leader

So how much of life science leadership is mechanistic and systematic? It is undoubtedly surrounded by supporting processes and enabling bureaucracy, but all of that seems merely to create space and time for the more important differentiated and added-value element of leadership. This latter element is anything but process-driven. It involves personally modelling culture and norms so as to effectively exploit the cognitive diversity in the workforce. It involves using highly personal skills to coach individuals and release their potential. And it is based on deeply held personal values and behaviours that they, as leaders, have to embody in the form of a visible, recognisable leader. None of these things can be reduced to efficient, semiautomated processes. Our fifth lesson is that life science leadership is intensely individual.

6 Subsidiarity is a contingent craft

How much direct control do Life Science Leaders have? It is an important question because the answer defines what they do. If they control their organisations tightly, with any significant decision being made by the leadership team and within the sight of the CEO, then the job of a Life Science Leader is detail-focused, technical and very operational. If they choose to allow most decisions to be made at a lower level – at functional, country or business unit level perhaps – then their job is more one of strategic coordination of those decisions. And not only is the nature of their job different, so is their span of control. Leaders who delegate more have less direct control but can govern a more diverse organisation, such as one spread across multiple therapy areas and geographies. Those who control more tightly are limited, simply by the number of hours in a day, to governing an organisation with tighter focus on fewer markets.

As with other aspects of leadership, the management literature, both academic and popular, is divided on whether leaders should be delegators or controllers. There are obvious advantages and disadvantages to each. Tight control, it is suggested, allows faster and more focused implementation of strategy, less contradiction or conflict between different parts of the business, more standardisation and therefore greater efficiency. The stereotype of a strong leader of a multinational corporation has her or him not only making the big strategic choices but also being acutely interested in the details of customer experience, product design and brand integrity. On the other hand, subsidiarity – the taking of decisions at the lowest possible level – is commended as enabling flexibility, adaptation to specific local conditions and making best use of employees' expertise. This stereotype has the leader as the enabler who trusts others to make it happen. Whatever their merits, both ideas tend to be normative, that is they say how leadership ought to be done, with relatively little consideration of how the choice depends on the situation.

Despite that, some of the leadership literature uses pharmaceutical and life science companies as examples; none of it pays much attention to the exceptional conditions that shape the industry, as discussed in Lesson I.

Because the answer dictates what leadership in the life sciences is and because there is no industry-specific research on the topic, I decided to ask my interviewees how they addressed the issue of subsidiarity. In short, their answer was that subsidiarity is a contingent issue; it depends on what the decision is and the context. More usefully, their answers revealed that much of the skill of leadership in the life sciences lies in understanding which decisions should be retained, which should be delegated and the implications of either delegating or retaining. What emerged were the interesting, valuable lessons that Life Science Leaders have learned as they decide on how much control to retain or let go and how to mitigate the risks inherent in their choices.

The need for subsidiarity

When Life Science Leaders discuss the need for subsidiarity, they talk in particular about two of the conditions that make the industry exceptional: workforce composition and complexity, both supply side and demand side, as described in Lesson I.

The disproportionately technically qualified, highly expert and mission-committed workforce of a typical life science company creates many implications for how they are led, prominent amongst which is their strong desire for autonomy. As Will McGuire noted, his firm needs educated, intelligent people and they work most productively when given autonomy and responsibility. He described his approach to doing this as "hire and trust". Gabriel Baertschi saw empowerment, which includes both autonomy, resources and direction, as a prerequisite for both effectiveness and agility. Kieran Murphy noted what he saw as a correlation between the independence given to units and their performance. None of this is surprising. The management literature associates autonomy with job satisfaction, reduced stress, performance and motivation, especially amongst knowledge workers. What was most interesting was that all of the interviewees talked about delegation in the context of clear direction and specific expectations. In this way, they differed from the "servant" school of leadership thought that allows for more self-setting of goals.

After workforce composition, the second factor that the interviewees saw as increasing the need for and value of subsidiarity was the complexity of the business. On the supply side, especially in larger firms with a diversity of therapy or business areas, the technological complexity of developing and making products stood out. Some interviewees cited how firms like GSK had attempted to manage this by splitting research and development up into relatively autonomous "centres of excellence". Others described the industry trend towards business units that separate businesses with different dynamics, such as mature and innovative products, or the splitting out of oncology and gene and cell therapies from more traditional business units. Still others noted how acquired companies, such as Genentech by Roche and Genzyme by Sanofi, were now often managed separately rather than integrated into the acquirer. Each of these is a type of approach to managing supply-side complexity by chopping it up and delegating the decisions to a lower level.

The demand-side complexity of the business was also seen as favouring subsidiarity. Deborah Dunsire saw greater subsidiarity in commercialisation decisions as a natural consequence of variability in local regulatory, market access, purchasing and usage conditions of national pharmaceutical markets. And, even though in the different category of medical technology, Jeroen Tas saw different market environments, such as their level of maturity and intensity of competition, as demanding decentralisation of decision making. Other interviewees spoke of the amount of discretionary activity involved in the exploitation of local market opportunities, which makes centralised control impossible. (See Lesson 2 and how the complexity of the industry requires mission-guided direction.) Yet others spoke of the "nature" of sales, marketing and other local commercial people as being especially demanding of autonomy and habitually resistant to centralised control.

The complexity of the industry requires mission-guided discretion

So, the life sciences industry has, more than most others, strong reasons to need and value subsidiarity. It is hard to imagine it being led in the same way as a simpler industry that may have a less expert workforce, such as retail or food and drink. If there were no other considerations, the life sciences industry would have a leadership style that defaulted to subsidiarity. But, of course, there are other considerations.

The value of retention

When Life Science Leaders talk of the need for centralised control, they again talk of the complexity of the business, but also of its exceptional longevity and scale of risk. It is clear that they value subsidiarity, but they also see the need to balance it. Yukio Matsui, for example, described combining local agility with global consistency as a core challenge for leaders in the life sciences industry.

The complexity of the life sciences industry creates an enormously difficult coordination task both within and between different stages of the value chain. In essence, this is the challenge of microcongruence – aligning internal functions with their colleagues – as discussed in Lesson 3. In some cases, the delegation of decisions hinders microcongruence, which Maurits Wolleswinkel pointed out when we discussed the problems of dispersed structures in his complex and highly technical business. Jeroen Tas, whose business has some similarities to that of Maurits, explained to me that the integrated nature of his product and service portfolio, and the way that value flows from the integration as much as the products themselves, means that decisions in product and service development really need to be centralised. So, complexity, especially of the supply side of the market, pushes leaders towards centralisation and retention of decisions.

The magnitude and longevity of risk also pushes Life Science Leaders towards retention of decision making and away from subsidiarity. When assets at risk are so large, technical and commercial uncertainty so great and risks are sustained for such a long time, the leadership team feels a huge responsibility not only to manage and mitigate that risk but also to demonstrate that risk management. As I'll describe in Lesson 7, they must not only manage risk but be seen to do so by their stakeholders. This ties in to the industry's social contract too. A product that fails commercially will damage a firm's finances and reputation with investors and partners but a product that causes harm, or a pricing strategy that seems exploitative, will have much greater consequences; it would threaten the industry's relationship with society. Some of the interviewees spoke of certain risks as being so large that they could "live nowhere else but in my office". So, magnitude and longevity of technical, commercial and reputational risk pushes towards centralisation and retention of decisions.

The life sciences industry has, again more than others, strong reasons to need and value centralisation of control. Again, it is hard to imagine decisions being made in this industry in the same way as a lower risk, less complex industry, such as consultancy services or fashion. If there were no other considerations, the life sciences industry would have a leadership style that defaulted to centralised control. But, as we have seen, there are other considerations.

The craft of contingency

As my interviews revealed, there are strong, compelling arguments to be made for both extremes of the control-subsidiarity spectrum. Simplistically, one might expect firms to choose an approach between these two ends of the spectrum. But the Life Science Leaders I interviewed were anything but simplistic thinkers and what emerged from the interviews was what can only be described as a two-stage craft of contingency: firstly, melding together various factors to decide the level of subsidiarity appropriate to each kind of decision, and secondly, taking steps to mitigate the risk that subsidiarity brings as the price for flexibility.

The purpose of choosing which decision is taken at what level is to resolve a tension, as Meinrad Lugan described, between the pressure to centralise, in order to achieve cost control and compliance, and the need for autonomy, so as to address local needs. As Louise Makin put it, this finely crafted choice, between how much control vs how much responsibility and accountability, is totally situational and cannot apply across all decisions in the business. Other leaders pointed to the situational factors that shaped that choice. Andy Thompson pointed to the role that geographical variation played as a "boundary condition" for the choice. Peter Stein, interestingly, described how the relatively narrow geographical focus of his business allowed more centralised decisions. Patrice Baudry described how, in his organisation, the criticality of decisions determined the choice between control and subsidiarity. Meinrad Lugan described something very similar in his description of how his firm differentiates between strategy-making decisions and strategy-execution decisions. Other interviewees gave examples of how this works in practice. Roland Diggelmann described a spectrum from centralised core decisions, such as those concerning new product development, to very local decisions, such as those regarding sales and marketing strategies, with some issues, such as pricing policy, straddling the two.

For decisions that were delegated to the lowest appropriate level, the second stage of the craft of contingency lay in the risk-mitigation steps. Unsurprisingly, all the interviewees pointed to the need for appropriate governance and approval processes to enable the accountability and responsibility of subsidiary units. Perhaps more surprisingly, our discussions also focussed on softer, cultural methods of mitigating the risks of subsidiarity. Jeremy Levin put subsidiary decisions in the context of the ethics of the company. I felt Jean-Christophe Tellier's phrase, "space with consistency" was a cogent way of describing how he helped subordinates to shape decisions. Taken in context, his comments were similar in meaning to Will McGuire's "hire and trust" dictum, mentioned earlier. It was consistent too with Lars Fruergaard Jørgensen's statement that he saw his role as to articulate corporate vision, not how to achieve it. What was most salient in this part of the interviews was that the interviewees were complementing governance processes with a significant reliance on soft, cultural methods to mitigate the risks of subsidiary decisions, even though those decisions often had far-reaching consequences. Again, it is useful to think of this blended choice – hard governance and soft culture – as an adaptation to the complexity of the organisation and the demands of the exceptionally expert workforce. It would be hard to craft hard rules that could cope with this level of complexity and, even if one did, they might be resisted by an expert workforce. A blended approach is a better fit to these industry conditions.

There was one more element to this leadership craft that came out of the interviews. This was the habit that Life Science Leaders have developed to mentally "let go" of decisions that were given to subsidiary units. Many of the interviewees described this as an essential behaviour. Patrice spoke for many of the interviewees when he told me he had developed the ability not to get lost in operations and to live with the fear of something going wrong. Kieran Murphy said that he tried not to worry too much and that to do so would hinder his ability to do his job. Michel Pettigrew told me that one had to be prepared to make mistakes. Similarly, Meinrad Lugan shrugged as he said one had to learn to live with minor errors. I felt this "learning to let go" was an important but implicit part of the craft of contingent subsidiarity. A leader who could not let go would have to fall back on centralised decisions.

Contingent subsidiarity: A leader's craft

So how much direct control do Life Science Leaders have? I had probed into this control-subsidiarity issue because it is central to how a leader leads. I found that the issue is especially important in the life sciences industry because its exceptional conditions create

7 Stakeholders demand consistent, transparent positioning

How do Life Science Leaders work with external stakeholders, such as shareholders and investors, payers, key opinion leaders, partner organisations and patient groups? It's an important question for two reasons. Firstly, working with these external shareholders is a large part of a leader's job. As the face of the company and a primary channel through which the company communicates with the outside world, the leader is the company. And, in that role, she or he is expected to be much more than a front or a figurehead; she or he must have a deep knowledge of the company's mission, goals, strategy and, at quite a detailed level, the mechanics of how it is executing its plans. Secondly, the company's relationship with those external stakeholders is often mission-critical. A bad relationship with any one of its many external stakeholders can damage the company severely. Such damage might be obvious, financial damage such as share price; but it might equally be less obvious long-term damage to reputation that influences who other companies choose to work with. What is more, in an age when every utterance is public and mistakes can spread around the world in moments, the external-facing role of the leader is arguably more difficult and more important than ever.

In the academic literature, there is little of any substance to answer the question of how leaders work with external shareholders. Much of what there is concerns CEO charisma or communication tactics and consists of normative, prescriptive instructions for how CEOs ought to behave. I found the general tone of this literature to be superficial, as if working with external stakeholders were more about presentation and spin than performance and science. Nor does this normative literature seem to fit well with the exceptional characteristics of the industry. What emerged during this part of my interviewing is that target audiences in the life sciences industry are sophisticated and the subject matter is complex, reflecting the industry's complexity. Further, the industry's goals are, and must be shown to be, more than returns on investor capital. In addition to any other goals, when a Life Science Leader works with external stakeholders, she or he must uphold the social contract that exists between society and the industry. As Andy Thompson so clearly put it, his firm does not do PR, it does science and engages with stakeholders on that basis.

Because of the importance of the question and my perception that published answers were inadequate, I set aside a whole section of each of my interviews to ask how my interviewees work with people and organisations outside their company. All the interviewees had clear and coherent views on the topic, which reflected the salience of this task to them. On careful analysis, these views coalesced into a single imperative: the need to develop, maintain and communicate a transparent and consistent positioning with external stakeholders, one that aligned what the company was doing with the goals of those stakeholders. That in itself was interesting; it refuted the idea that their job was to be a charismatic communicator, a well-paid spin-doctor. And, beneath that simple answer lay a mass of interesting valuable lessons that Life Science Leaders had learned about how to work with external stakeholders.

Complex audiences and conflicting views

All companies in all industries have external stakeholders but the complexity and difficulty of external-stakeholder relations varies with their products and their markets. Companies such as Starbucks, who sell simple products directly to consumers, have a relatively simple task, to use an extreme example. By contrast, the life sciences industry lies at the other extreme of this spectrum because, in comparison to other industries, its range of stakeholders and the depth and richness of interaction that it is necessary to have with them, is exceptional.

In addition to the traditional targets of external relations, such as investors and the media, the life sciences industry must consider a number of other constituencies too. These include a triumvirate of "customers" – patients, healthcare professionals and the payers who authorise payment for products. In addition, the nature of the industry demands relationships with governments and its agencies, such as regulatory bodies and health technology assessors. And that is only to consider the demand side of the business. In many cases, external relations also include development partners, such as universities and smaller technology firms, contract manufacturers and research organisations and distribution partners. Typically, the value chain of a life science company is less like a chain and more like a web of allied organisations. In my other work on the evolution of the industry, I call it a holobiont, comparing it to the complex interconnectivity of a coral reef.

The relationship with each of these groups is rich and complex. In many markets, the patient audience includes their family. Sometimes, the channel of communication is through patient advocacy groups. Healthcare professionals are stratified, ranging from global and national opinion leaders to established professionals to trainees. They include not only doctors but many other professionals ranging from nurses to laboratory scientists. Payers operate at local, national and, increasingly, international levels. As a global business, company interactions with regulators occur at national, regional and global level. Through this dense web of participants, the information that must flow is both highly technical but also varied, ranging from scientific data to clinical recommendations to health economic data. And all these interactions must be compliant with the law, regulation and industry codes of behaviour, which often vary between countries and between different classes of products. In reality, the picture is even more complicated than this, but this sketch serves to make the point: communication with the external stakeholders of the life sciences industry is too complex and too rich to be a matter of spin.

My interviewees knew that I understood the industry well, so their comments quickly moved beyond the fact of this complexity and on to its implications. These stem from the divergent proximate objectives of each external shareholder and, to a degree, their different world views. Jeremy Levin stressed that it was imperative to recognise the different perspectives of different external stakeholders. Patients and prescribers want products that are ever more innovative and effective. Regulators want minimal risk. Payers want optimal outcomes for the lowest possible cost, whilst maintaining diversity of supply. These goals often contradict each other. As Will McGuire noted, even though healthcare professionals and payers are "on the same side", it is sometimes difficult to reconcile their needs. In addition to these customer expectations, the demands of all kinds of customers are potentially in conflict with the goals of business owners and investors, who seek an economically sustainable business model. What is more, as if these potential tensions were not difficult enough, there is significant heterogeneity within each group. Investors have differing aims according to their portfolio goals, patients and professionals have differing needs according to their clinical situation, regulators have different standards, and payers vary in how narrowly or broadly they define value. There are even cultural differences, as Maurits Wolleswinkel described when he talked about the different perspectives of US and European healthcare systems.

Meanwhile, underpinning all this complexity is a tension that exists in few other industries: that between a mostly commercially-oriented supply side and an often public or not-for-profit demand side. This brings with it differing world views on the role of profit and private capital. Finally, these complex, conflicting requirements operate over the very long term. As Namal Nawana pointed out, CEOs must manage the conflict between short-term reporting cycles and longer-term innovation cycles. And the needs of each external stakeholder are evolving at different speeds over time, as Stephen Moran observed when he talked about how value-based healthcare was gradually, unevenly co-evolving out of co-operation between life science companies and payers.

In summary, the simple "charismatic communicator" picture seems a totally inadequate description of what Life Science Leaders must do when they engage with external stakeholders. To revert to my evolutionary metaphor, the life sciences environment would strongly disfavour that approach, rendering spin-doctor CEOs extinct. Instead, what emerged from my further questioning and analysis was an altogether more interesting picture.

Three steps to managing external stakeholders

The almost overwhelmingly complex nature of this external-stakeholder relations task was the first thing to emerge from my questioning in this area. Inevitably, it prompted me to probe deeper into how Life Science Leaders deal with this Gordian knot. As before, my interviewees' rich and thoughtful answers gelled during analysis, this time into a three-step answer.

Step 1: Recognise that we share ultimate goals

At an almost visceral level, my interviewees wanted to stress that, beneath the differing and contradictory needs of external stakeholders lay a more fundamental and honourable truth that is arguably unique to the life sciences industry: all stakeholders share the ultimate goal of saving or improving human life. Jeroen Tas captured the gist of all the interviews when he talked about the mission of his organisation – striving to make the world healthier through innovation – as being something that he could easily agree on with all his external stakeholders. As another example, Allan Hillgrove emphasised the effort he and his colleagues put into making stakeholders appreciate that their mission is to create both economic and societal value. Peter Stein talked about the difference between firms like his, who seek to create long-term value for all stakeholders, and others, who might only seek to extract cash from the business and the market. Jean-Christophe Tellier told me how important it was to remember that all of his firm's many stakeholders share the same ultimate aim, even if their immediate aims differed. I especially warmed to Louise Makin's passionate beliefs as she told me that the special thing about the life sciences industry is that it can, through innovation, create new value that can and should be shared amongst all stakeholders. I concluded that this elucidation and agreement of a common ultimate goal was the starting point for how Life Science Leaders engage with external stakeholders.

Step 2: Be consistent and transparent about our position

An obvious potential cause of tension between a life science firm and its external stakeholders lies in the heterogeneity of the latter and the fixed nature of the former. Simply put, the complexity of a life science company means that it cannot shift from, for example, being a low-cost, low-risk, low-return business to the opposite in the short or even medium term. To all practical purposes, it can only be the sort of business that it is. The consequence of this inflexibility is that life science companies have learned the value of adopting a consistent, transparent positioning with their stakeholders, that is maintained over the long term. All of the firms I interviewed, for example, adopted a position with investors of "we'll deliver risk-adjusted returns appropriate to an innovative life science company, not those of another sector". Will McGuire was emphatic about the need to be honest about his firm's positioning with investors when he described "spin" as a slippery slope. Patrice Baudry told me that he had learned that capital markets value transparency and that, especially during periods of change, it was essential to communicate clearly to investors. Roland Diggelmann spoke of the need for a clear and consistent narrative with investors, regulators and other external stakeholders. Jeremy Levin nicely summarised the view of all my interviewees regarding investor relations when he described it as keeping trust by delivering your promises and allowing investors to decide where, if at all, your firm fits in their investment portfolio.

It was particularly interesting that the same consistent and transparent positioning principle was just as applicable to customers and other stakeholders as to investors. For example, all my interviewees' firms adopted a position that could be approximated to "we'll deliver fairly priced innovation, not low-priced imitation". Both Michel Pettigrew and Allan Hillgrove described their efforts to be transparent with patient advocacy groups. Jane Griffiths attributed the need for transparency, not only on pricing but also for example on trial results or payments to healthcare professionals, to the need for healthcare companies to be especially trustworthy. Yukio Matsui illuminated the pressures of the regulatory and social environments, making it ever more important to preserve a trustworthy reputation, something which he felt could only come from transparency. A particular view on this was given by both Jeroen Tas and Maurits Wolleswinkel when they talked of how dependent their businesses were on long-term collaboration with leading clinicians, and how that also depended on a transparent and consistent positioning in the market place. So, after elucidating and agreeing shared goals, Life Science Leaders' second step in working with external stakeholders is to adopt a clear position with respect to how they intended to achieve those goals, and to substantiate that position by consistent and transparent behaviour.

Step 3: Manage your risk portfolio transparently

The first two steps described above – shared ultimate goals and consistent, transparent positioning – seem to be necessary but insufficient for working with external stakeholders. As I probed further, a third necessary step emerged from the analysis: to demonstrate that the risks associated with the stated goals and position were managed and mitigated as much as possible. It became clear that this was at the core of communicating with all external stakeholders because, directly or indirectly, much of what the interviewees talked about concerned managing risk and showing they had done so. This lesson is clearly an adaptation to the exceptionally high and long-term technical and commercial risks that characterise the industry, as discussed in Lesson 1. The management of this risk is important to all stakeholders, not only investors, because the consequences of poor risk management would affect them all. It would lead to ineffective or harmful products, high costs and low returns. As Jane Griffiths told me, the risk and uncertainty in developing medicines is so great that a firm must demonstrate that those risks have been managed as well as possible. This point was made in many other interviews too. Namal Nawana cleverly illustrated the link to the sustainability of his business when he described effective risk management as earning the right to make future investments.

The finding that demonstrable risk management was the third essential step to managing external stakeholders inevitably led to me probing for how Life Science Leaders did this. Those questions revealed that it was a matter of portfolio and process.

Large life science businesses rarely take single risks; they typically have a portfolio of projects. Meinrad Lugan explained to me that, in order to get a better understanding of overall risk and the synergies between projects, it is important not to look at risks in isolation but to look at decisions within that portfolio of risks. Peter Martin put it another way. His firm manages risks by the way they fit with other risks, what management scientists call complementarity. This portfolio-of-risks approach is so embedded that when I asked Roland Diggelmann about how he managed a single risk, he looked puzzled by my belief that risks were ever managed in isolation. In similar tone, Kieran Murphy told me that his business was not about taking risks or being cautious; it was about managing a portfolio of risks diligently.

How life science firms manage their portfolio of large and long-lasting risks is also a matter of process. The firms I interviewed varied in the details of this. Gabriel Baertschi talked about new models of risk management evolving, with risks being shared with collaborators and, in some cases, with customers. More traditionally, all the Life Science Leaders interviewed talked about transparent processes for ensuring that their technical and commercial risks were demonstrably managed. Jane Griffiths talked of the value of using external expertise in evaluating clinical risk. Lars Fruergaard Jørgensen described his "triple bottom line" conversation with shareholders and its value in shifting perceptions of risk, for example those arising from the entry of biosimilars into his market. Other interviewees spoke of variations of balanced scorecards and metrics dashboards and procedures for making scientific decisions transparent and traceable. The common thread in all their comments was that the exceptional magnitude and longevity of risk in the life sciences industry makes the management of that risk exceptionally important to external stakeholders, so requiring that it be both effective and transparent. Every stakeholder is vulnerable to the industry's exceptional risk, so every stakeholder is exceptionally interested in it. They vary only in which area of risk they focus on.

So, demonstrable risk management joins defining shared goals and adopting a consistent, transparent position as the third necessary condition for effective stakeholder management.

Here I stand, transparently and consistently

So, how do Life Science Leaders work with external stakeholders? This part of my research led me through what all research scientists will recognise as a U-shaped journey of discovery. I began with a working hypothesis, formed from the literature, that their role was best described as a "super-spokesperson," someone whose charisma and communication skills could spin their company's message in different ways to satisfy the divergent desires of their various stakeholders. My hypothesis crumbled as I began to understand the horrendously heterogenous and apparently irreconcilable demands of investors, patients, professionals, payers and partners. It only recovered when three shared views emerged from my interviewees' answers. First, have a common goal. Second, adopt a consistent and transparent position with respect to that goal. Third, use the portfolio and processes to manage the inevitable risks of that position as well and as demonstrably as possible.

Following these three steps does not obviate the need for good communication skills, but it provides a much more realistic picture of how Life Science Leaders engage with external stakeholders. As these lessons emerged, the attitudes of my interviewees with respect to their external shareholders reminded me of Martin Luther's famous statement in defence of his position: Here I stand, I can do no other. That is the seventh lesson of leadership in the life sciences.

8   Words are important

Have Life Science Leaders learned to use words in a particular way? It is an obviously important question, since a leader's facility with language is likely to be a fundamental skill. But it was not a question in my interview script. I had chosen what questions to ask, based on reading the leadership literature and four decades working in and then researching the life sciences industry. How leaders use language had not arisen as a topic to explore, perhaps because it is so essential and elemental. That it did so was partly due to my training as a researcher but also because of something Louise Makin said. My training has taught to me to listen for dissonance in interviewees' responses; not contradictions so much as "key changes" that indicate the interviewee has, usually unconsciously, moved from one mode of thinking to another.

Louise Makin, who came across as both formidably competent and charmingly authentic, had just told me, with strident emphasis, how the level of control her leadership team chose to exert, rather than delegate, was completely dependent on the situation (see Lesson 6), implying significant flexibility and adaptability of style. Shortly afterwards, she mentioned how she had a "stock of phrases" that she found useful to use repeatedly when communicating internally. This suggested a certain routinisation of her behaviour that was at odds with her normally flexible style. It was only a small point, but I scribbled "cog diss" (short for cognitive dissonance) in my notebook to remind me to think about it. Later, as I sat in the coffee shop below her London office going through my notes, it occurred to me that Louise had revealed a pattern not only in her behaviour but in the interview data overall, one that I had not realised was there. Louise was one of the last of my interviews and all of them had shown a similar pattern: an extensive tendency to use figures of speech and other rhetorical devices to make their point. My interview notes were rich in metaphor and simile, allegory, imagery and in manufactured memorable memes, some of which were copied and others original. Despite its salience, I had not seen this shared habit until Louise's "key change" had triggered my training and alerted me to it. Life Science Leaders do use words in a particular way; they are especially fond of crafting figures of speech, very deliberately, to use them as tools.

The language instinct

Steven Pinker, the Canadian cognitive psychologist, talks of humans having a hard-wired instinct for language. It is an innate tendency to choose words and phrases that influence how our listeners think in a given context of our thoughts and theirs. As I listened and re-listened to the recordings of my interviews, I began to see that my interviewees had particularly well-developed language instincts, which they were using to adapt to the peculiarities of their leadership situation.

There are several aspects of a Life Sciences Leader's situation that favour or disfavour different modes of language usage. The first of these is the complexity of the ideas they need to communicate. This includes not only the deep technical complexity of subject matter that these leaders must deal with, but also the enormous variety of different subjects, from clinical data to health economics and from legal compliance to sales performance. The second aspect was that much of what they have to say contains, superficially at least, internal contradictions, such as when they must communicate the need for urgency and diligence at the same time. A third factor is that their position of authority sometimes causes their words to be misconstrued, such as when they suggest latitude around goals but are interpreted as demoting the importance of those goals. A fourth aspect of their situation is that they often need to drive change against a heavy inertia of existing culture and systems, for example when responding to major shifts in the market. Fifth, their communication is often indirect, through layers of management. Sixth, their communication is often very time-constrained, such as conference addresses or short calls. Finally, their verbal communication is only one channel that must be complementary to and congruent with a mass of written communication.

These various conditions make for a demanding communication environment. In the absence of a control study from another industry, my research cannot claim that a Life Science Leader's communication task is more demanding than that of her or his peers in other industries, but the exceptional conditions of the industry imply that it might be. Both the difficulty of communicating well and the risks associated with not doing so must be greater than for most other industries. It would be unusual then, and counter to the evolutionary view of how organisations change, if Life Science Leaders had not adapted their use of language to their particular communication environment.

The uses of language

Armed with this new hypothesis, that Life Science Leaders have adapted their use of language to fit the particularities of their communication environment, I revisited my interviews to look for examples of how this worked in practice. Was there some pattern or method to how they did it and to what ends? Sure enough, the recordings were replete with figures of speech. On analysis, these fell in to a small number of usage categories.

To express subtlety of meaning

One of the challenges facing Life Science Leaders is the way their position distorts how others hear what they say. Whereas one may interpret a peer's words in context and allow for some non-literal subtlety of meaning, a leader's words can often be taken literally, like a fundamentalist interpretation of a religious text. In the communication context described above, this can be difficult to overcome but, in my interviews, I saw many varied examples of figures of speech being used to adapt to this problem.

Deborah Dunsire, for example, was explaining the necessity and importance of allowing subordinates to make mistakes from which they learned. She clearly had the challenge of communicating that errors were permissible whilst, at the same time, conveying that this shouldn't involve big mistakes with irreversible consequences for the company or the individual. To communicate this, she spoke of it being "ok for people to stub their toes". It was a very effective metaphor, perfectly balancing the pain of the mistake with the tolerable acceptability of the consequences. Jane Griffiths did something similar when she was trying to convey just the right balance between doing a job well and not becoming an ineffective perfectionist. She spoke of being comfortable with things "fraying at the edges a little". Again, the effectiveness of this expression lies in its balance of negative (fraying) and positive (at the edges a little). Perhaps my favourite example was Andy Thompson's, when he explained how he communicated the subtle differences in priority between the commitment of employees, customers and investors. He compared it to air, water and food. Being without any of these will result in death, but lack of air, like lack of employee commitment will kill you quickly. Lack of water, like lack of customer commitment, will kill you quite soon afterwards. Lack of food will surely kill you, like lack of investors, but only later. Andy's turn of phrase was one that communicated the subtle interrelationship between three main stakeholders quite beautifully.

All three of these figures of speech, and many others in the interviews, did their job perfectly. But it is only when one considers how one might convey the same messages in formal language, and how lengthy and open to misinterpretation that might be, that it becomes clear how well these figures of speech were adapted to the particular context of the life sciences communication environment.

To reify an intangible idea

The life sciences industry has a strongly scientific culture, one that epistemologists would call logical positivist. For all its other benefits, this culture disfavours ideas that are not or cannot be evidenced in hard data. As a result, good intangible ideas can lose out to weaker but quantified ideas. Obviously, an environment in which weaker ideas win over stronger ideas is problematic. Life Science Leaders therefore use figures of speech to support intangible ideas.

Jean-Christophe Tellier provided a good example of this. He wanted to communicate his belief that an individual's efficacy was the result of finding a role that aligned perfectly with her or his natural talents. It's a well-studied phenomenon and he might have resorted to peer-reviewed academic proofs, but he didn't. Instead, he told an allegorical story of his time in training when he worked with an exceptionally productive and skilled orthopaedic surgeon. The efficacy of the surgeon was the result of the alignment of his job and his natural talents. The allegory was effective because we can all understand easily how difficult orthopaedic surgery is and we can all respect the surgeon. Interestingly, in this case the anecdote was much less scientifically rigorous, in a logical positive sense, than the available published data about efficacy and job-fit. But Jean Christophe understands the power of a good story in reifying an intangible idea.

Meinrad Lugan used a very different story to similar effect. We talked in a hilltop office with beautiful views overlooking a valley, nestling in which was his company's factory. He wanted to convey that, even in the absence of intellectual property protection, it was hard for competitors to imitate what they did because of the large amount of tacit knowledge inherent in their manufacturing excellence. This idea of inimitability without intellectual property rights is hard to communicate in an organisation as rational as his. So he described to me an event that, I am sure, he has described many times to his colleagues. In his telling, potential rival companies are allowed to look around the factory, even at the risk of observing something that could help them imitate and compete. But this does not happen. Instead, rivals observe the intricate, detailed efficiency of the factory and decide that it would be too hard to imitate, choosing instead to compete with less competent rivals. It is a wonderful story because it is both counterintuitive and perfectly believable. Like Jean-Christophe, Meinrad understands how a good story can outweigh the obviously rational.

Both stories worked in similar allegorical ways. The anecdotes are easy to grasp and their conclusions are hard to argue with. As a result, the intangible idea becomes more concrete in the mind of the listener.

To clarify contradictory complexity

One of the by-products of the life sciences industry's complexity is that it sometimes generates ideas that are, or can appear at first sight to be, internally contradictory. Most of us struggle to work with ideas that appear to contradict themselves. This is the origin of F. Scott Fitzgerald's famous observation that the test of a first-rate mind is the ability to hold two opposed ideas at once and still function. In particular, the industry's social contract and complexity inevitably create opposing ideas, arising from the need to address the sometimes-conflicting needs of a triumvirate of customers and sustain the business at the same time. Again, the interviews revealed that Life Science Leaders use figures of speech and rhetorical devices to resolve this contradictory complexity.

Jeroen Tas illustrated this technique of clarifying complexity perfectly. Creating sophisticated medical equipment systems, his company's value proposition is especially complex, even in comparison to, say, a pharmaceutical company. And that value proposition needs to create more than one kind of value for patients, payers and a variety of professionals. To communicate this potentially contradictory set of goals, Jeroen and his colleagues speak of their "Quadruple Aim" of clinical outcomes, patient experience, professional experience and health economic value. The idea works because it is a laudably succinct summary of a very complex web of goals and, as used eloquently by Jeroen, perfectly communicates the parity, as opposed to a hierarchy, of the four objectives.

Kieran Murphy used another metaphor to communicate a slightly wider example of resolving contradictory complexity. Whilst a number of the interviewees spoke of the patients' needs as being a guiding star, Kieran went two better. He described steering his organisation relative to three stars: company purpose, business objectives and their position in the industry. Steering by any one of these alone would be disastrous, he said, and his words painted a vivid picture of a ship's captain triangulating his position against three fixed stars. This metaphor works because it is easy to imagine the image, and three reference points are intuitively more reassuring than only one. Kieran could have simply spoken of three goals, but the imagery is a much stronger means of communication.

Once more, we have two figures of speech that differ in detail but perform the same role. In these cases, they take complex arguments that could easily be seen as being inherently contradictory and turn them into something that is easy to communicate and understand.

To implant a memorable meme

In 1976, Richard Dawkins coined the term meme for an element of culture or behaviour that is passed from one individual to another. In doing so, he introduced the world to the equivalence between memes and genes and their shared struggle to survive and propagate. Although the term has now been debased to mean some piece of social media content, the original meaning of memes remains important and that is the sense in which I am using it here.

In life science companies, an obvious feature of the communication environment is the intense competition amongst memes. We see this in everything from legal instructions to comply with regulation, to a short-term sales team exhortation to push to the end of the quarter. Any message, even those from the most senior leaders, must penetrate and embed through this cacophony of other messages, each of which might well be louder and more immediately pertinent to the recipient. Life Science Leaders appreciate this and have adapted their use of language accordingly in order to implant their meme in the memory of their audience.

Many Life Science Leaders use traditional techniques of rhetoric to cut through this noise. Two of these include the tricolon (using three parallel words or phrases in succession) and alliteration, and both of these are used frequently in all public speaking. A particularly strong example of it was given by Namal Nawana who described how he communicated his organisation's core values to its employees. Many companies have long and unconvincing value statements but Namal's is just three words: Care, Collaboration and Courage. These are elaborated upon, but it is this alliterative tricolon that implants the meme. In this case, it is the classical use of two rules of rhetoric that makes the meme so memorable.

I was also struck by Maurits Wolleswinkel's use of language to implant a meme about self-management. His aim was to encourage colleagues both to work hard under pressure and to rest and refresh themselves. To do so, he used the metaphor of an athlete working and recovering, and he drew out the point that it is the alternation of intense work and genuine rest that allows athletes to build their strength. The image stayed with me and I am sure it does with Maurits's colleagues. It works because it is a clear, easy to understand metaphor that feels intuitively obvious and because the parallels between work and athletic performance are so clear.

The two examples differ, but they both use language to communicate and implant an idea that might otherwise be lost in the noise.

The language of the heart

Thus, a topic that was not even on my agenda at the beginning of my research eventually became one of the significant findings of it. Life Science Leaders characteristically use language in a particular way. They do so in order to adapt to their communication environment, which is the result of the industry's exceptional characteristics. They use figures of speech and rhetorical devices in many different ways but with four particular aims in mind. They do this as an indispensable complement to more formal channels of written and other communication because even the expert workforce of life science companies are humans that enjoy figurative language. As these conclusions emerged from my data, I was reminded of the words of Nelson Mandela, who said "If you talk to a man in a language he understands, that goes to his head. If you talk to him in his language, that goes to his heart." This is the eighth lesson that Life Science Leaders have learned.

9 Protect the leadership asset

How do Life Science Leaders sustain their productive capacity? It is an important question because, although part of a leadership team, the individual abilities and capacities of the Life Science Leader are vital to the organisation's effectiveness. If their productive capacity is compromised, through physical or mental health issues, reduced vitality or for any other reason, then that will be reflected in their organisation's performance. And, since leading any large organisation is physically and mentally taxing, sustaining the leader's productive capacity is a significant concern. There is no evidence to suggest that the life sciences industry is exceptional in this respect, but it seems likely that its complexity, workforce composition, social responsibility and risks (as described in Lesson 1) make it at least as demanding as other sectors. Because of this, I decided to ask my interviewees about how they maintain their ability to function at this high level.

In the management literature, it is taken as given that senior leaders must maintain their productive capacity. But research on how they do this does not go far beyond obvious platitudes of delegation, physical health and time-management that might apply to any manager. Search for how leaders stay productive in practice and there is little beyond the prescriptive, normative listicles that do not recognise differences between either individuals or their situations. Given this paucity of research generally, it is unsurprising that there is nothing specific to the productivity of Life Science Leaders. It is not, of course, certain that this issue is industry specific; Life Science Leaders may only face the same issues as their peers in other sectors. But, given the exceptional industry characteristics that shape the industry, I wanted to investigate whether the industry context made a difference. What emerged is that how Life Science Leaders sustain themselves and their productive capacity is indeed coloured by the industry's exceptional conditions.

The mission tilts work-life balance

I began my questions about maintaining productive capacity by asking about work-life balance. My study was neither comparative nor quantitative. Instead, I was interested in how subjectively satisfied my interviewees were with the division of their time between work and non-work activity.

What emerged first from the analysis is that Life Science Leaders are both committed to work-life balance whilst at the same time being sceptical of the concept. The interviewees saw a balanced life as both personally important and essential to productivity, but they were keen to qualify the idea. From their perspective, the concept of work-life balance risks being thought of too simplistically and their combined answers sought to qualify the concept in three important ways. Firstly, any senior role involves a level of commitment, of both time and energy, that is a long way from the norm for most people; so work-life balance must be considered in the context of the role. Secondly, the balance point between work and life is a very personal and dynamic choice, varying over time and with personal circumstances such as family life stage; there can be no such thing as universally appropriate work-life balance. Finally, and perhaps most specific to the industry, my interviewees' personal and emotional investment into the mission of their organisation influenced their perception of what a good work-life balance was.

This last point, that work-life balance is tilted when your work is so important to your life's goals, came out in many of the interviews. I recall that Maurits Wolleswinkel pulled a slight, involuntary grimace, as if I had asked a slightly naïve question. He then patiently explained to me that he saw work-life balance as less a simple equilibrium of hours and more a symmetry of satisfaction between different spheres of life. In the same vein, Will McGuire spoke of his experience of hearing patients describe how his company's products had changed their lives and how that made him feel he was doing good rather than just earning a salary. Lars Fruergaard Jørgensen spoke of his deep personal involvement which meant that, although he enjoyed a healthy out-of-office life, he felt he never could or wanted to "take off my CEO hat". Peter Stein spoke very movingly of how his sense of responsibility to his firm, its employees and patients meant that his life and work blurred into each other in a satisfying, fulfilling way.

Overall, the interviewees spoke of their work-life balance as a constant challenge, one that could never be conclusively resolved but with which they felt satisfied because they felt they were doing meaningful, socially valuable work. It is worth remembering at this point that many of the interviewees were trained as healthcare professionals and even those that were not had spent many years engaged with the industry's social contract. From this part of our conversations, I concluded that Life Science Leaders' view on work-life balance is not the same as in other industries; it is uniquely coloured by one of the industry's exceptional features – its social purpose – influencing how Life Science Leaders see their lives.

Notwithstanding this industry-specific view of work-life balance, there remains the challenge of trying to maintain it, so my questions went on to ask how they approached this. As ever in qualitative interviews, a torrent of varied, unstructured answers eventually resolved, on analysis, into three broad categories.

First, build your submarine

One of the points that most of the interviewees made was that their role could, if not managed well, create a level of pressure that was unbearable by any human being. They ascribed this pressure not only to a very high work volume, which is presumably not specific to the industry, but also to intense emotional involvement in the nature of the work, which may well be. Many interviewees spoke of their feeling of responsibility, the needs of the patients and of the potential for good or harm inherent in their decisions. I was left without any doubt that this emotional involvement contributed to the pressure associated with their role in a way that I had not seen in other industries.

As I studied their answers, the first point to arise was that the interviewees try to limit the pressure on themselves to an amount that is sustainably manageable. There was an especially strong agreement between the interviewees' answers on this subject which, on analysis, resolved to four distinct types of pressure-reduction behaviour.

The first is the creation and use of a supportive team of assistants and immediate reports. This seems to go far beyond a merely competent group of subordinates. Patrice Baudry, for example, spoke of the benefits of trust between his executive committee colleagues, which created a less pressured environment. Louise Makin stressed the importance of her immediate colleagues understanding and allowing for her strengths and weaknesses. The common theme here was that building and using a supportive team was the first priority in maintaining productive capacity; without that team, the role would overwhelm anybody.

The second pressure-reduction behaviour is the ability to prioritise effectively. Whilst this seems obvious, their approach to prioritisation was different from those recommended in text books. Rather than prioritise tasks according to their importance and urgency, several interviewees described an approach to prioritisation based on the importance of the decision to the company and the contribution the leader could make personally to the decision. Jeroen Tas spoke of focusing where he personally could make a significant contribution. Michel Pettigrew described prioritisation in terms of both his own focus and delegating to appropriately skilled colleagues. In a reminder of the social mission of the industry, Russell Mably referred to using the mission to set his personal priorities consistently, so avoiding short-term exigencies. The common theme in this case was the need to focus the leader's limited time on what no one else could do.

Complementing prioritisation, interviewees described a third pressure-reduction behaviour of not worrying about things that had been delegated to others. Jane Griffiths talked of developing a tolerance of "letting things fray at the edges just a little" whilst Meinrad Lugan described how he had gradually learned to accept small errors. Roland Diggelmann emphasised the need to trust his team to execute what had been delegated to them, without monitoring too closely. The shared idea in all these responses was that prioritising and delegating to a supportive team is of little value if one still holds on to the task mentally.

The final pressure-reduction technique is proactivity. Slightly paradoxically, several interviewees argued that actively engaging with tasks reduced pressure in comparison with reactive "firefighting". Lars Fruergaard Jørgensen made this point especially forcefully, linking stress with the need to react to events. Jeroen Tas made a similar point when he described his proactivity as the habit to "drive for impact" and the benefits that brought him.

As I listened to the recordings of my interviewees, I began to appreciate the pressure they are under. Some of these would be felt by any CEO in any industry, but Life Science Leaders have the additional pressures created by the exceptional conditions of the industry. As an adaptation to these pressures, they build a metaphorical submarine to protect themselves and, so great is the pressure, its hull must have four layers, the four behaviours described above.

Even with this protection, the pressures on a Life Science Leader are high and sustained, so next I probed for what they do to sustain their productivity under pressure. The answers again showed that, although at a general level their behaviours probably apply to any senior business leader, the specifics are adaptations to the industry context.

Physician, heal thyself

Researchers are trained to look beyond the obvious and to weigh every piece of evidence, even the apparently trivial. I met most of the interviewees in person and those that I could interview only remotely I saw in photographs as I read their biographies. This provided a very unexpected source of evidence. For a sample based on industry and role, one might have expected a variety of physical body types representative of the middle-aged people that they all were. But this was not the case. My interviewees were disproportionately lean and physically fit. Given their demanding jobs and travel-intensive lifestyles, I was very surprised by this so I probed for any habits that might explain this. What emerged was an acute awareness that what Louise Makin called "the leadership asset" was housed in a human body, with all its mental and physical fragilities, that must be protected. The focus on maintaining mental and physical health was quite remarkable. Or at least it seems so until one considers that many of the interviewees were either medically trained or had spent their careers working in the healthcare field. In short, what I saw in these inordinately healthy leaders was the corollary of working lives dominated by the needs of very unhealthy people.

Although their backgrounds explained the priority they gave to their own health, it left another obvious question unanswered. How do they stay fit and healthy given their long working hours, extensive travelling and the temptations of business dinners? Their answers, which fell into categories of mental and physical health, are interesting to those who might want to emulate them.

With very few exceptions, all the interviewees exercised regularly and significantly, but what was most interesting was the self-discipline with which they achieved this. Meinrad Lugan described his morning regime of swimming before breakfast. Louise Makin lives near her London office during the week, but the weekends find her sailing competitively off the south coast of England. Yukio Matsui chooses hotels with gyms. Maurits Wolleswinkel packs his running gear on business trips. Lars Fruergaard Jørgensen shares my interest in cycling. Many others, like Namal Nawana, talked of how they had transitioned from playing team sports to individual activities, such as running, that they could opportunistically squeeze into business trips. As I listened to the interviewees, it was clear that they had learned to treat exercise not simply as a leisure activity, to be fitted in when time allowed, but as an item on their to-do list, to be conscientiously scheduled alongside other tasks that had the same, not greater, priority.

Whilst many interviewees saw their physical exercise as contributing to their mental health, I was also interested to know what other methods they adopted to stay mentally capable of their roles. Some of the answers were unsurprising. A strong, supportive family life seems important and, for example, Andy Thompson kindly met me at a hotel where his family were gathering en route to their winter holiday. Kieran Murphy was typical when he stressed the importance of sleep. Allan Hillgrove revealed his habit of grabbing sleep on short flights. But perhaps more surprising were the more idiosyncratic habits some had developed to sustain their mental health. Stephen Moran was among several who practised meditation. Maurits Wolleswinkel and others recommended periods of disconnecting from emails and messages, for example in the evening. Will McGuire's personal recommendation was to spend some time each day reviewing tasks, priorities and goals. Like physical exercise, the interviewees had developed personal habits to sustain mental health and strength that were suited to their situation. Despite this individuality, a common theme did emerge – focus. Despite the pressures to do otherwise, when these extremely busy people are not working, they focus on what they are doing as strongly as when they are working. When they are with family and friends, when they are exercising, listening to music or reading a book, they sustain their mental health by focusing on that for the restoration of their mental energy.

Protecting the leadership asset

For most of the time I spent talking to these Life Science Leaders, we discussed how they made best use of their firms' assets: their intellectual property, their expert workforces and their brands and corporate reputations. They saw themselves as custodians of those assets and worked hard to build and maintain them. When we moved on to talking about how they sustained their own productive capacity,

I realised that they looked at their physical and mental health and strength through the same lens. They themselves are part of the leadership asset and they have a responsibility to protect that asset, just as if it were a patent or a factory. That responsibility translates into a discipline, for most of them, of physical exercise that many have ingeniously adapted to a life of meetings, aeroplanes and hotels. The same discipline extends into setting aside time for family, friends and emotionally nourishing activities that they focus upon and defend against the encroachment of their work life. Protecting the leadership asset is the ninth lesson these Life Science Leaders have learned.

10 Leadership is a growth process

What would Life Science Leaders say to their younger selves? It is an important question because it captures what younger executives in the life sciences industry might learn from the successful, experienced and estimable leaders that they aspire to emulate. If, as Lesson 1 argues, this industry is exceptional, then it follows that the wisdom acquired from my interviewees' aggregate experience (I estimated that they cumulatively represented approximately 600 years of learning) will be of more direct relevance to them than the generalised, prescriptive cant one finds in many books on leadership.

"What advice would you give to your younger self?" was the last question I asked during my interviews. It also appeared to be the hardest to answer. Answering the preceding questions, my interviewees were characteristically confident of their answers. They were obviously comfortable answering questions about, for example, how to deal with external stakeholders or facilitate their leadership team. But when I asked this final question, they almost all responded in the same revealing way. They often sat back in their chairs, exhaled, sometimes laughed and frequently asked for time to think about the answer. Many of them self-deprecatingly joked that they were not sure they had learned much at all. When they did answer, it was with thought, care and modesty. I could almost see them picturing their younger selves. As expected, their answers were very varied in detail but, when analysed, they crystallised into five broad kinds of advice to themselves as they started their career.

To thine own self be true

The job of a Life Science Leader is arguably more demanding than that of her or his peers in other industries because of the exceptional conditions that characterise this industry. Its social contract demands an unusual level of emotional involvement. The depth and breadth of its complexity would stretch anyone's intellect. Its expert workforce makes leadership anything but a routine, mechanical activity. And all these factors are amplified by the magnitude and longevity of the risk involved.

In the face of the physical and mental demands of such a role, one of the topics that emerged strongly in this part of the interviews was the adherence to personal values. This was not surprising; there is a substantial body of academic research about this. Studies show that, especially for knowledge workers whose jobs have a high discretionary content (see Lesson 2), it is difficult to sustain commitment and performance if the job involves violating one's personal values.

It was not surprising to hear the interviewees talk about personal values, but the emphasis they placed on them when asked what they would tell their younger selves was remarkable. Deborah Dunsire described leadership itself as a "fundamentally value-based" activity. Although each described it in their own words, most of the other interviewees said something similar. Gabriel Baertschi said unequivocally that the first thing he would tell his younger self was "be ethical, always". Jeremy Levin was concerned that avarice sometimes threatened to undermine or distract executives in the life sciences industry from their personal values. Consequently, his lesson for his younger self was not to confuse money with integrity. The tone and emphasis of many of the interviewees made me think that, during their careers, many of them had heard a siren call to abandon their personal values but had learned to resist it. Overall, I came to realise that adherence to personal values was important to Life Science Leaders not only in its own right but also because it allowed them to act authentically and therefore sustainably in this demanding industry. In Kieran Murphy's words, you need to be able to act as if someone important is watching you, even if they are not, and to feel that you are doing the right thing. Writing up my notes in the Amersham café opposite Kieran's office I scribbled two lines. The first was C. S. Lewis's definition of integrity, that it is doing the right thing even when no one is watching. The second was Polonius's line from Hamlet: "To thine own self be true." Whether or not my interviewees knew these words at the start of their careers I don't know, but these are certainly the first lesson that they would choose to pass backwards in time to their younger selves.

Be helped towards your true vocation

After authenticity and adhering to one's own personal values, I asked my interviewees what career guidance they might give their younger selves. They had each had what most people would consider a fantastically successful career path, so I was interested to know if there were any transferable lessons they might share. Something in my question might have suggested I was looking for a quick and easy answer, because they almost all wanted to make clear that success had no short cuts and there was no substitute for hard work and perseverance. Their answers implied that their experience found this to be a lesson that some people need to learn. But taking that very important point as a given, I probed for more counterintuitive lessons and two revealed themselves.

The first was that, as Louise Makin described it, you should allow yourself to be drawn to what excites you, rather than be attracted by the superficial attractions of title, salary and status or held back by lack of confidence or self-belief. Russell Mably added another dimension to the same idea when he advised his younger self to pick something you love and to which you can make a significant contribution. Will McGuire and others spoke of how choices they had made very early in their career had influenced their future careers more than they anticipated at the time. In this context, many of the Life Science Leaders cautioned against underestimating one's own potential. Namal Nawana told his younger self not to limit his sense of adventure. Jean-Christophe Tellier advised young people to think of their capacity as infinite. Jane Griffiths told me that her current position would surprise her younger self because she never expected to proceed so far. As I listened to the interviews, it seemed that they were all telling their younger selves to think of their vocation rather than their careers.

The second lesson that emerged frequently was how much career progression depends on the help of others. Several interviewees talked about their luck in finding supportive, nurturing managers to work for and advised young people, where possible, to choose their bosses wisely. Others spoke of the value of their wider networks of colleagues and peers in different organisations. Jean-Christophe Tellier cautioned against underestimating how important personal relationships are in sustaining a career. Patrice Baudry advised his younger self not to neglect his wider professional network and to be generous in helping others because altruism of that kind is, eventually and indirectly, rewarded. Still others spoke of the value of mentors or personal coaches. Gabriel Baertschi told his younger self that mentors were very valuable but that one has to develop the skill of listening to them and using the wisdom they pass on. The common theme in all of the interviewees was that finding and following one's vocation is not something one could do alone.

These two nuggets of Life Science Leaders' advice to their younger selves are especially valuable when contrasted with the mindset of many early career stage executives. In my work with younger managers, I often see them ignore their calling in their pursuit of a prestigious title. Through their words I hear them describe career progression as a selfish, competitive activity. I have no idea if my interviewees held these views in their younger lives, but it was obvious that they now see career progression as the opposite – as working co-operatively towards an innately-dictated vocation by seeking and accepting the support of others.

Constantly sharpen your saw

The third topic around which my interviewees' answers coalesced was that of their personal learning and development. It was clear that they saw their careers as a growth process, enabled by an ability to be self-critical, of constantly working to fill gaps in their own knowledge and skills. Because this was a very individual process, the examples of personal development they used were very varied. Some advised themselves to fill their critical knowledge gaps sooner, as Michel Pettigrew did when we discussed his scientific knowledge. Others wanted to tell their younger selves what particular skills they had learned that had been especially useful. In Gabriel Baertschi's case, this included the skill of hearing, through the "noise" of market research, "signals" about what really drives the market. Several others talked of developing the skills of critical thinking, such as identifying implicit assumptions or embedded cognitive biases. Still others talked about personal attributes that they wish they had learned sooner. I empathised with Gabriel Baertschi when he advised his younger self to learn patience sooner. Russell Mably returned to the pervasive importance of sincere empathy as an attribute to be honed.

Whatever the individual specifics of learning and self-development, it became obvious to me that, with hindsight, the Life Science Leaders could look at their younger selves and see their own weaknesses. And what they had learned, despite the pressures of everyday tasks, was to focus some of their energy on their own personal growth, what Stephen Covey called "sharpening the saw".

Be reflectively confident

One line of my interview questions asked about self-doubt, self-confidence, where the appropriate balance between the two lay, and what they might tell their younger selves about how to find that balance. The interviewees were of a mind that confidence, not to be confused with arrogance, was a necessary attribute for a Life Science Leader and some spoke of seeing others paralysed by lack of this trait. They described the way in which they found the right balance in different ways. Roland Diggelmann spoke of allowing enough time to listen and reflect but, in the end, "trusting his gut". Louise Makin similarly described, after all due thought and analyses, following her intuition. Many of the interviewees, however, qualified this need for intuitive confidence with a counterbalancing need for humility, reflection and self-awareness. I was fascinated to hear both Deborah Dunsire and Kieran Murphy, among others, observe that confidence was less an innate personality trait and more the result of careful thought and humility about the limits of one's own knowledge. Meinrad Lugan also provided another insight when he revealed that his wider interests and experience of life helped him be aware that every decision could be looked at from different perspectives.

This outcome of my interviewees' experience seemed to me to be an especially valuable lesson for younger managers. It made me recall seeing less competent managers either paralysed by indecision or arrogantly decisive. It seems that walking the line between these two, being reflectively confident, is extremely difficult but that it is something my interviewees had learned to do.

Enable others' greatness

As we continued to discuss what my interviewees might say to their younger selves, the fourth topic that emerged was concerned less with their own development and more with the development of others. A common theme was the value of helping others to learn, grow and achieve their potential. Interestingly, although there was sincere kindness in their words, these comments were not made in a purely benevolent tone. It would be more accurate to say that they were, in the phrase of evolutionary psychologists, a lesson in reciprocal altruism. That is, these Life Science Leaders had learned that enabling others to succeed is a very effective way of ensuring one's own success. Jeremy Levin spoke with a passion about enabling people by giving them direction, resources and the necessary skills to achieve their goals. Jean-Christophe Tellier was similarly motivated by the part of his role that involved helping others to fulfil their potential. Russell Mably described how he had learned the value of being approachable and empathetic in helping his colleagues to develop. Maurits Wolleswinkel put a slightly different complexion on the same idea when he talked about the value of recruiting and developing people to have skills that complemented those already in the team.

As they revealed this fourth lesson to their younger selves, the interviewees often sounded maternal or paternal in their tone. Indeed, Andy Thompson compared the challenge of being simultaneously warm, authentic and authoritative when coaching others with the challenges of fatherhood. After he had left me in a noisy London hotel bar, to join his family and begin his holiday, I sat for a moment and reviewed my notes from our conversation. At the bottom of the page, I wrote a phrase that he had reminded me of, one that is usually attributed to Ronald Reagan: "The greatest leader is not necessarily the one who does the greatest things. He is the one that gets the people to do the greatest things."

A lifetime of learning

What would Life Science Leaders say to their younger selves? In the interviews, I was a little surprised when this last question caused a shift from confident, pre-considered answers to hesitant, self-deprecating comments. It seemed out of character for these powerful, successful people. But when their comments coalesced during analyses, I understood the reason for this change. Follow your vocation, constantly build your capabilities, balance confidence and thought, and support others' growth are all very useful advice for younger executives. The hesitancy of the answers was not because they felt they had nothing to offer. It was because they all felt they were, even in their senior positions after decades of experience, still learning themselves. That leadership is a lifelong growth process is the tenth lesson of Life Science Leaders.

Conclusion

The science of leadership

The book is written primarily for those who work in the life sciences industry and are inquisitive about, and perhaps aspire to, leadership in this fascinating and important business. But this book is only part of the output of a much larger body of work. For the last 21 years, I've been trying to understand how this industry evolves, a curiosity created by the preceding 20 years of my career, as a research scientist and then marketer in pharmaceutical and medical technology companies. In this bigger project, part of my work at Bocconi and Hertfordshire Universities, I apply the concepts of Darwinian evolution to understand how and why life science business models change. In Lessons 1 to 10, you will have detected hints of that Darwinist approach but, for the most part, I've avoided talking about the science of how leadership can be seen through an evolutionary lens. This final chapter, however, is aimed at those readers with a more scientific bent. Its aim is to help you understand some of the science beneath leadership in the life sciences.

The evolution of the life sciences industry

Please don't misunderstand me when I use the term evolution. I do not use the word in its simple, everyday usage, meaning gradual change without any specific mechanism. When I use the word evolution, I mean it in the scientific, Darwinian sense of the term: a process of change within a population, the mechanism of which involves the variation of individual traits, selection for or against those traits by the environment and amplification of those favoured traits by replication.

We're most familiar with this Darwinian use of the word in biology but, as Stanley Metcalfe observed, evolution is not only biological theory, it's just that the biologists got there first. In fact, scientists from many disciplines use evolutionary theory to explain the behaviour of complex adaptive systems. I am simply a management scientist who uses it to explain the complex adaptive system that is the life sciences industry. That said, the quickest way to understand how Darwinian evolution applies to any industry, including the life sciences industry, is to begin with a very simplified reminder of how it works in biology.

In biology, we call a group of organisms with the same traits a species. You, for example, are a member of a species characterised by a big brain, walking upright and talking. Those traits are the result of your many biological processes and those processes are enabled and driven by your many proteins. The collective term for these proteins, of which you have about 90 million working away in your body, is your proteome. Your proteome is made by (more correctly, expressed by) its genome, which is the collective term we use for your roughly 20,000 genes. And each of your genes is a long sequence of As, Cs, Ts and Gs, the biologists' shorthand for the bases adenine cytosine, thymine and guanine.

Evolution, in the Darwinian sense, occurs when those base sequences vary. Those variations create mutated genes, which therefore express different proteins, which cause changes in biological processes and lead to different traits. The environment favours or disfavours those new traits, giving the mutant a reproductive advantage or disadvantage. Advantaged mutations out-multiply their disadvantaged cousins and gradually a new group of organisms, all sharing the same advantaged traits or traits, emerges. When that happens, we call it a new species. That is how you and I, with our big brains and other traits, got here.

With humble apologies for such a coarse simplification, that is how evolution works in biology. At its heart is variation of, and selection for, the information-storing, replicable entities we call genes, which evolutionary scientists call replicators, and their environment-interacting vehicles, which are called interactors.

Now consider the very direct analogy between biology and business. We call a group of organisations with the same traits, such as their products, structures and strategies, a business model. Those traits are the result of organisational processes, which are enabled and driven by the organisation's capabilities. An organisation's entire complement of thousands of capabilities is called its capabileome. Each capability is the expression of many organisational routines, the many small, stable subprocesses that every organisation has. For example, your organisation probably has routines for specifying a new product, doing market research or segmenting the market. An organisation typically has many thousands of routines and they are created by aggregations of what are known as microfoundations. There are four kinds of microfoundations:

- The attributes of the individuals performing the routine, such as their knowledge, skills and other personal characteristics
- The structure, composition and connectivity of the groups performing the routine
- The processes that go on within the group in order to perform the routine
- The methods used to manage conflict and co-operation within and between the groups performing the routine

In my book *Darwin's Medicine*, where these ideas are explained at much greater length, I managed to contort the abbreviation of these four microfoundations into ACTG for the very good reason that they are the direct analogues of the bases adenine, cytosine, thymine and guanine.

Evolution of an industry, in the Darwinian sense, occurs when these microfoundations vary. This changes the organisation's routines, which changes its capabilities, which changes its business processes and leads to different organisational traits, such as products, structure and strategy. The market and competitive environment then either favours or disfavours those changed traits, giving the "mutant" organisation a competitive advantage or disadvantage. Companies that succeed are imitated by successful rivals, who mimic their microfoundations, routines, capabilities, processes and traits. As a result, a new group of companies emerge, all sharing the same competitive traits. When that happens, we call it a new business model. Simply put, that is how evolution works in business. At its heart is variation of the information-storing, reproducible entities we call organisational routines and their market-interacting vehicles we call companies. And just as, to a biologist, genes are replicators and organisms are interactors, to a management scientist like me, routines are replicators and organisations are interactors.

Despite the greatly simplified picture given here, the parallels between evolution in biological systems and in economic systems are direct. What we observe in the life sciences and other industries is not *like* Darwinian evolution, it *is* Darwinian evolution. I am drawing an analogy, not using a metaphor. This evolutionary perspective on business is, I should stress, not a personal whim. It has been well established amongst academic researchers since 1982, when Nelson and Winter published their seminal work *An Evolutionary Theory of Economic Change*. To the best of my knowledge, however, my research group at the University of Hertfordshire is the only one applying this perspective specifically to the life sciences industry.

A Darwinian view of leadership

Just as evolutionary biology informs almost every aspect of how we understand the living world, a Darwinian perspective on how industries change has very wide applications. In my previous books, such as *The Future of Pharma* and *Darwin's Medicine*, I've concentrated on how evolution shapes strategy and structure and leads to the speciation of the life sciences industry into 26 different business models. The value of a strong theory is that it can be used to make sense of many different phenomena. In other work, I've used it to explain the way that brand strategy is adapting to a different market environment. This book, however, takes a Darwinian view of leadership and that view opens two lines of research. Firstly, what selection pressures are acting on leadership practice in the life sciences industry? Secondly, how have the routines and microfoundations of leadership adapted in the face of those selection pressures?

As I discussed in Lesson 1, the life sciences industry has four exceptional characteristics:

- Both the supply and demand sides of the market are unusually complex, involving the interrelation of many domains of knowledge at a very high level.
- The magnitude of both tangible and intangible the assets at risk is very large and those risks persist for decades.
- The industry's workforce is exceptionally expert, being composed of a very high proportion of well-qualified and experienced knowledge workers across many disciplines.
- The industry has an implicit but well-understood contract with society that accepts profit making from human adversity in return for accessible, effective therapies.

As a management scientist with an evolutionary perspective, I look at these conditions as selective pressures, in much the same way that a biologist with an evolutionary perspective might look at climate change or pollution. Just as, for example, marine biologists have found that certain species of fish in Mexican rivers have adapted to sulphurous spring water, I'd expect to see leaders in life science companies adapting to these four industry characteristics. Likewise, as my biologist colleagues would look for changes in the proteomes, genomes and base sequences of those fish, I'd expect to see adaptations in the capabilities, routines and microfoundations of Life Science Leaders, as these four factors act, both individually and in aggregate, to favour and disfavour certain traits of leadership.

This kind of research requires an open mind; it is essentially inductive research that looks at the qualitative data to see what emerges, rather than a deductive method that tries to support or refute preformed hypotheses. But this kind of research also benefits from what Louis Pasteur called a prepared mind; it helps if you have a broad idea of what to look for. In the same way that my biologist peers would expect to see certain physiological adaptations to cope with sulphur, I would expect to see adaptations in leadership.

- Adaptation to complexity that enable the collation, synthesis and application of many diverse sets of advanced knowledge regarding both supply and demand sides of the industry
- Adaptations to risk that enable the management of large, long-term risks of various kinds in a way that is demonstrable to multiple external stakeholders
- Adaptations to expert workforces that enable that direction and motivation of a workforce with an exceptionally high proportion of well-qualified and experienced knowledge workers across many disciplines
- Adaptations to a social contract that enable the adherence to the social contract whilst simultaneously maintaining an economically sustainable business

In this work, such adaptations do emerge. Lessons 1 to 10 are adaptations to the four selection pressures acting on Life Science Leaders. Because my research sample was successful leaders of successful companies, those I interviewed were those who had adapted whilst those who had not adapted were outside of my sample.

Adaptations to complexity

The collation, synthesis and application of many diverse sets of advanced knowledge, ranging over both supply and demand sides of the industry, is a formidable selection pressure. It is especially so because of the inherent tension between achieving microcongruence and macrocongruence at the same time, as discussed in Lesson 3. The recognition of bicongruence as the central issue, and the subsequent framing of the leadership task as essentially a bicongruence task, is an adaptation to this selection pressure. In particular, we can look at the three approaches described in Lesson 3 (selecting and managing for organisational salience, focus on microcongruence and nurturing of trust) as routines that have evolved in order to achieve bicongruence. In the same way, the Decisive Facilitator role discussed in Lesson 4 is another adaptation to complexity and the five steps described in that lesson can be seen as "mutated" routines that have been selected for by the leadership environment. The demands placed on leaders by this complexity lead to Lesson 9, routines to protect the leadership asset, and the environment's dynamism leads to routines for constant growth, as described in Lesson 10. Peering beneath these adapted routines, we can see microfoundations of leadership in the life sciences industry. A good understanding of the science, the ability to set one's own ego aside, methods for optimising integrative conflict and breaking down problems are all examples of microfoundations that make decisive facilitation and the achievement of bicongruence possible. Prioritisation of one's own mental and physical health and a learning mindset are among the microfoundations needed to protect and to grow the leadership asset.

Adaptions to risk

The management of various large, long-term, technical, economic and reputational risks, and the demonstration of that risk management to multiple external stakeholders, is another selection pressure that is especially characteristic of the life sciences industry environment. At its root lies our incomplete knowledge of the fundamental science, and the tension between the proximate interests of the various stakeholders. The most obvious adaptation to this pressure is that described in Lesson 7, regarding the firm's positioning to stakeholders. The capability to adapt is made possible by the steps described in that lesson (establishing shared goals, transparent, consistent communication, portfolio approaches), which are themselves collections of many organisational routines. Those routines are underpinned by microfoundations including attributes (such as "appetite for risk"), group processes (such as those for working with investors) and conflict management methods (such as the time taken to explain pricing to payers and patients). But we can also see the use of mission statements, Lesson 1, as a supporting adaptation to the risk environment because of the way it complements the corporate positioning. Adherence to the mission is also enabled by its own accompanying microfoundations, such as acting ethically and with integrity. Without these microfoundations, the firm's ability to survive this high-risk environment would be weakened.

Adaptations to expert workforces

The direction and motivation of a workforce with an exceptionally high proportion of well-qualified and experienced knowledge workers, across many disciplines, is one of the less obvious but more powerful selection pressures on the industry. It is amplified by social trends, such as the "death of deference" and higher societal expectations for autonomy and diversity. So powerful is this selection pressure that we can see evidence for it in four of the lessons: 2, 5, 6 and 8. Clearly, the exceptional importance of the mission (Lesson 2), is an adaptation to employees who seek to form affective commitment to their employers. In Lesson 5, the importance of coaching and appreciation of cognitive diversity are also adaptations to this exceptional workforce composition. The craft of contingency (Lesson 6), is clearly a capability developed to balance the value of retention against the demands for autonomy. And the use of language described in Lesson 8, is selected for by the need to communicate complex, sometimes contradictory, information to intelligent, critical employees. In these lessons, we see the development of various routines, such as in coaching, delegation or crafting language. And these routines are made possible by microfoundations such as empathy, governance processes and acuity for choice of words. As with the other adaptations, we see the adaptive response to the workforce composition reflected ultimately in the microfoundations of leadership.

Adaptations to the social contract

Adherence to the social contract whilst simultaneously maintaining an economically sustainable business, is arguably the selection pressure that is most unique to the life sciences industry. It has been amplified in recent years by higher social expectations, demographically driven demand and the economic implications of new therapies and technologies that are at once innovative and very expensive. This selection pressure can be seen in many of the lessons in the book. Crafting and using the mission, as discussed in Lesson 2, is the most visible adaptation to the pressures of the social contract. The management of the triumvirate of patients, professionals and payers, part of Lesson 7, is another set of capabilities that are selected for by this pressure. The use of words (Lesson 8), is in part demanded by the need to visibly comply with the contract in a very public sphere. And ultimately, adherence to that contract is impossible without bicongruence (Lesson 3), which is largely achieved by decisive facilitation (Lesson 4). Beneath all these adapted capabilities and routines lie microfoundations, such as emotional commitments to patient outcomes, groups dedicated to improving access and beliefs that reconcile profit and public good. Adaptation to the pressures of the social contract are pervasive throughout the life sciences industry because those firms that failed to adapt to this pressure have not survived.

A complex, adapting system

These four snapshots, each of which sees the lessons in this book as evolutionary adaptations to the particular conditions of the industry, are of course simplifications. In truth, every lesson in this book is an adaptation to all four pressures acting at once. But simplifications have their merits. In this case, it helps us see that the ten lessons are not separate, unrelated observations of how Life Science Leaders behave. They are better understood as ten adaptations to the selection pressures acting on the industry, pressures which flow from the industry's specific characteristics. Unlike other books that prescribe normative leadership behaviour across any industry, this book should be seen as carrying the opposite lesson: good leadership can't be prescribed; it is a matter of understanding and adapting to the leadership context. That is the lesson of leadership in the life sciences.

Index

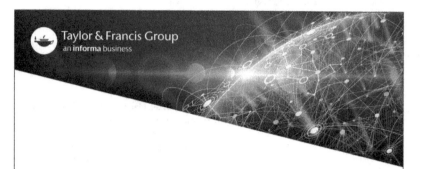